Role and Attribute Based Access Control (RBAC/ABAC)

James Relington

DEDICATION

This book is dedicated to all the professionals and organizations dedicated to strengthening cybersecurity and protecting valuable data. Your commitment to building secure, efficient systems is inspiring, and this work is for those who continue to innovate, learn, and adapt in the ever-evolving field of access control.

vi

AKNOWLEDGEMENTS

I would like to express my sincere gratitude to all those who supported and encouraged me throughout the creation of this book. Special thanks to my colleagues and mentors, whose insights and expertise shaped many of the ideas presented here. I am also grateful to my family and friends for their patience and unwavering support. Lastly, I would like to thank the readers who are dedicated to enhancing their knowledge and improving access control practices in their organizations—this work is for you.

Introduction to Access Control

Access control is a fundamental concept in cybersecurity and information systems, determining who can access specific resources, what actions they can perform, and under what conditions. It plays a crucial role in protecting sensitive data, ensuring compliance with regulations, and maintaining the integrity of digital environments. Without proper access control mechanisms, organizations expose themselves to risks such as unauthorized data breaches, privilege escalation attacks, and operational disruptions.

At its core, access control revolves around the idea of restricting or granting permissions based on predefined rules, policies, or contextual conditions. The process begins with authentication, where an entity—be it a user, application, or device—proves its identity. This is typically done through passwords, biometric verification, security tokens, or multi-factor authentication (MFA). Once authenticated, the system moves to the authorization phase, where it evaluates whether the authenticated entity has the necessary permissions to access a specific resource. This evaluation is based on access control policies that define what is permissible and under what circumstances.

The need for access control stems from the increasing complexity of modern IT environments. Organizations manage vast amounts of data distributed across on-premises systems, cloud infrastructures, and hybrid networks. Employees, third-party vendors, customers, and automated systems all require access to different resources, often from various locations and devices. This complexity makes it essential to implement robust access control mechanisms that can dynamically adapt to changing security requirements while maintaining usability and efficiency.

Historically, access control mechanisms have evolved alongside technological advancements. Early systems relied on discretionary access control (DAC), where resource owners determined access permissions. While flexible, DAC was prone to misconfigurations and security loopholes. Later, mandatory access control (MAC) introduced a more rigid structure where access was enforced based on predefined policies, often used in military and government environments. Role-based access control (RBAC) emerged as a widely adopted model, assigning permissions based on predefined roles within an organization. More recently, attribute-based access control (ABAC) has gained popularity by allowing access decisions to be made dynamically based on attributes such as user identity, device security posture, location, and time of access.

Effective access control implementation requires striking a balance between security and operational efficiency. Overly restrictive policies can hinder productivity, causing frustration among users who require legitimate access to perform their tasks. On the other hand, overly permissive access control can expose critical assets to unauthorized entities, increasing the risk of data breaches. Organizations must regularly assess and refine their access control strategies to align with their business objectives while maintaining a strong security posture.

Access control mechanisms are also closely tied to regulatory compliance. Many industries operate under strict regulations that mandate how data should be protected and who should have access to specific types of information. For example, the General Data Protection Regulation (GDPR) in the European Union requires organizations to implement appropriate access controls to protect personal data. Similarly, the Health Insurance Portability and Accountability Act (HIPAA) in the United States mandates stringent access controls to safeguard healthcare records. Failing to comply with these regulations can result in severe financial penalties and reputational damage.

Modern access control strategies leverage advanced technologies to enhance security and adaptability. Zero Trust Architecture (ZTA) is a security framework that challenges the traditional perimeter-based approach by assuming that no entity should be trusted by default, even if it is inside the network. In a Zero Trust model, access control is continuously verified using dynamic policies that consider multiple contextual factors, such as user behavior, device health, and network conditions.

Artificial intelligence (AI) and machine learning (ML) are also transforming access control by enabling automated anomaly detection and adaptive access decisions. These technologies analyze patterns in user behavior to identify suspicious activities, such as unusual login locations or attempts to access unauthorized resources. By integrating

AI-driven insights, organizations can implement risk-based access control policies that dynamically adjust permissions based on real-time risk assessments.

Despite its importance, access control remains a challenging aspect of cybersecurity. One of the common challenges is the proliferation of shadow IT, where employees use unauthorized applications and services that bypass established access control policies. This can introduce security gaps, making it difficult for IT teams to enforce consistent access policies. Additionally, managing access for a diverse and ever-changing workforce, including remote employees, contractors, and temporary staff, requires continuous monitoring and policy adjustments.

Access control is not a one-time implementation but an ongoing process that requires regular audits, policy reviews, and technological updates. Organizations must adopt a proactive approach by continuously assessing their access control mechanisms, identifying potential vulnerabilities, and implementing improvements. By doing so, they can mitigate security risks, ensure compliance, and provide users with seamless yet secure access to necessary resources.

As technology continues to evolve, so will the methods used to enforce access control. Organizations must remain vigilant, embracing new models and technologies to stay ahead of emerging threats. Whether through traditional RBAC, flexible ABAC, or cutting-edge AI-driven access control, the ultimate goal remains the same: ensuring that the right people have access to the right resources at the right time while preventing unauthorized access that could compromise security.

The Evolution of Access Control Models

Access control has been an essential aspect of information security for decades, evolving alongside technological advancements and organizational needs. As systems have grown in complexity, access control models have adapted to ensure that sensitive information remains protected while still being accessible to authorized users. The development of these models has been driven by the increasing sophistication of cyber threats, regulatory requirements, and the growing need for more flexible and scalable security solutions.

In the early days of computing, access control was rudimentary. Systems were primarily standalone, with minimal need for complex security mechanisms. Access was managed through simple username-password combinations, and security was largely based on physical access to the machine. If an individual could physically access the computer, they could interact with its data and resources. This approach worked in environments where computers were isolated, but as networking expanded and systems became interconnected, more sophisticated access control models became necessary.

One of the first structured models to emerge was discretionary access control (DAC). In DAC systems, the owner of a resource had the discretion to grant or deny access to others. This model provided flexibility, allowing users to control access based on their needs. However, it also introduced security risks, as users could unintentionally—or maliciously—grant access to unauthorized individuals. Additionally, DAC often struggled with enforcing organization-wide security policies since access decisions were decentralized and could be inconsistent across different users and departments.

To address the limitations of DAC, mandatory access control (MAC) was developed, primarily for military and government applications where strict security policies were required. Unlike DAC, where users had control over access permissions, MAC enforced security policies centrally based on predefined classifications. Resources and users were assigned security labels, and access was determined by comparing these labels against established security policies. This rigid structure significantly improved security but lacked the flexibility needed in many commercial and enterprise environments. The complexity of implementing and managing MAC also made it impractical for widespread adoption outside of high-security environments.

As businesses and organizations sought a more structured yet flexible access control model, role-based access control (RBAC) gained prominence. Introduced in the 1990s, RBAC focused on assigning permissions based on organizational roles rather than individual users. Under this model, users were assigned roles corresponding to their job functions, and each role was associated with a predefined set of permissions. This approach simplified management by reducing the number of individual access decisions required and ensuring consistency across the organization. RBAC became widely adopted in enterprise environments, particularly in industries with strict compliance requirements such as healthcare, finance, and government.

Despite its effectiveness, RBAC introduced new challenges, particularly in dynamic environments where users frequently changed roles or required temporary access to specific resources. The rigid nature of RBAC often led to role explosion, where an excessive number of roles had to be created to accommodate different user needs. Managing these roles became a burden, prompting the search for more adaptive access control mechanisms.

Attribute-based access control (ABAC) emerged as a solution to the limitations of RBAC. Unlike RBAC, which relied on predefined roles, ABAC made access decisions based on attributes associated with users, resources, and the environment. Attributes could include user characteristics (such as department, clearance level, or job title), resource classifications, and contextual factors like time of access or device security posture. This model allowed for fine-grained, dynamic access control that could adapt to changing circumstances. ABAC provided greater flexibility and scalability, making it particularly suitable for modern cloud-based and distributed environments.

The shift toward cloud computing, mobile access, and decentralized workforces has further influenced the evolution of access control. Traditional models that relied on predefined roles and static policies became insufficient in an era where employees, contractors, and third parties needed access from various locations and devices. Zero Trust Architecture (ZTA) emerged as a modern approach, rejecting the assumption that internal networks are inherently trustworthy. Instead, ZTA enforces continuous verification of users and devices before granting access to resources. This model integrates principles from both RBAC and ABAC while incorporating additional security measures such as risk-based authentication, behavioral analytics, and real-time policy enforcement.

Artificial intelligence and machine learning have also begun to shape the future of access control. By analyzing user behavior and access patterns, AI-driven systems can detect anomalies and automatically adjust access policies based on risk assessments. For example, if a user suddenly attempts to access sensitive data from an unusual location, the system may prompt for additional verification or temporarily restrict access. These advancements are making access control more adaptive and proactive, reducing the reliance on static policies that may become outdated or ineffective over time.

As access control models continue to evolve, organizations must balance security, usability, and compliance. No single model fits all scenarios, and many enterprises are adopting hybrid approaches that combine elements of multiple models to achieve optimal security. The transition from simple password-based access to sophisticated, AI-driven adaptive controls reflects the growing complexity of modern IT environments and the increasing threats they face.

The evolution of access control has been shaped by the need to address emerging security challenges while maintaining operational efficiency. From the early days of discretionary access control to the modern implementation of AI-driven adaptive policies, each stage of development has built upon the lessons of the past. Organizations must stay vigilant, continuously evaluating and refining their access control strategies to keep pace with technological advancements and evolving threats.

Understanding Role-Based Access Control (RBAC)

Role-Based Access Control (RBAC) is one of the most widely used access control models in enterprise environments. It provides a structured and scalable way to manage permissions by assigning users to roles that define their access rights. Instead of granting permissions directly to individual users, RBAC groups users based on their job responsibilities, ensuring that access is consistent, manageable, and aligned with organizational policies. This model is particularly beneficial in large organizations, where manually managing access for hundreds or thousands of users would be inefficient and prone to errors.

The core principle of RBAC is that access is determined by a user's role within an organization. Each role is associated with a predefined set of permissions that dictate what actions the user can perform and which resources they can access. For example, in a hospital setting, a doctor might have access to patient medical records, while a receptionist may only be able to view appointment schedules. By structuring access around roles rather than individual users, RBAC simplifies administration, reduces security risks, and ensures that users have the appropriate level of access for their responsibilities.

RBAC is built on three primary rules that guide how access is granted and managed. The first rule is role assignment, which states that a user must be assigned to at least one role to gain access to resources. The second rule is role authorization, ensuring that users can only assume roles for which they have been explicitly authorized. The third rule is permission authorization, meaning that users can perform actions only if their assigned role includes the necessary permissions. These rules create a controlled and auditable access management system that minimizes the risk of unauthorized access.

A key advantage of RBAC is its ability to enforce the principle of least privilege. This security concept dictates that users should have only the minimum level of access required to perform their tasks. By defining roles with specific permissions, organizations can prevent employees from accessing sensitive data or critical systems that are not necessary for their job functions. This reduces the risk of accidental or intentional misuse of access privileges, which is a common cause of security breaches.

RBAC also facilitates separation of duties, a security measure that ensures critical tasks are divided among multiple users to prevent fraud or errors. For example, in a financial system, the role of entering transactions should be separate from the role of approving them. By enforcing separation of duties through RBAC, organizations can mitigate the risk of internal threats and maintain compliance with regulatory standards.

Despite its benefits, RBAC is not without challenges. One of the most common issues organizations face is role explosion, which occurs when too many roles are created to accommodate various exceptions and special cases. This can lead to an overly complex and difficult-to-manage system, defeating the purpose of RBAC's simplicity. To avoid role explosion, organizations should carefully design role hierarchies, consolidate overlapping roles, and regularly review role definitions to ensure they remain relevant and manageable.

Role engineering is a crucial step in implementing RBAC effectively. This process involves analyzing job functions, identifying common access requirements, and defining roles that align with business processes. A well-designed RBAC system requires collaboration between IT, security teams, and business units to ensure that roles accurately reflect real-world responsibilities. Organizations often use role mining techniques, which involve analyzing existing access patterns to identify common role groupings and optimize role definitions.

RBAC is also highly beneficial for compliance and auditing. Many regulatory frameworks, such as GDPR, HIPAA, and SOX, require organizations to implement strict access controls and maintain detailed audit logs. Because RBAC centralizes access management and enforces consistent policies, it simplifies compliance with these regulations. Auditors can easily verify that users have appropriate access and that changes to roles and permissions are properly documented.

Modern organizations often integrate RBAC with identity governance and automation tools to streamline role management. Automated provisioning ensures that new employees are assigned the correct roles when they join an organization, while de-provisioning removes access when they leave. This reduces the risk of orphaned accounts, which occur when former employees retain access to systems they no longer need. By integrating RBAC with identity and access management (IAM) solutions, organizations can enhance security, improve efficiency, and maintain compliance with industry standards.

As organizations move toward cloud-based environments, RBAC continues to evolve. Cloud platforms and software-as-a-service (SaaS) applications increasingly support RBAC, allowing organizations to extend role-based permissions across their IT infrastructure. However, the dynamic nature of cloud environments presents new challenges, such as managing access across multiple platforms and ensuring that roles remain aligned with evolving business needs. Some organizations adopt a hybrid approach, combining RBAC with more flexible models like attribute-based access control (ABAC) to accommodate complex access scenarios.

RBAC remains a foundational access control model that provides structure, security, and scalability. By defining roles based on business functions and enforcing consistent access policies, organizations can reduce administrative overhead, strengthen security, and improve compliance. While challenges such as role explosion and evolving business requirements must be carefully managed, a well-implemented RBAC system offers significant advantages in securing enterprise environments. As technology continues to evolve, RBAC will likely remain a key component of access management strategies, adapting to new security challenges and integration needs.

Understanding Attribute-Based Access Control (ABAC)

Attribute-Based Access Control (ABAC) is an advanced and flexible access control model that grants or denies access based on attributes rather than predefined roles. Unlike Role-Based Access Control (RBAC), which relies on static role assignments, ABAC evaluates various attributes related to users, resources, actions, and the environment to determine whether access should be granted. This dynamic approach allows organizations to implement more granular and context-aware access control policies, improving security and adaptability in complex IT environments.

ABAC operates on the principle that access decisions should be made based on a comprehensive set of attributes rather than predefined role memberships. Attributes can be categorized into four main types: user attributes, resource attributes, action attributes, and environmental attributes. User attributes define characteristics of the individual requesting access, such as their job title, department, security clearance, or device type. Resource attributes describe the asset being accessed, including its classification level, owner, or sensitivity. Action attributes specify what type of operation is being performed, such as read, write, delete, or execute. Environmental attributes consider external factors such as time of access, geographic location, device security posture, and network conditions.

By leveraging these attributes, ABAC allows for more nuanced and adaptable access control policies. For example, an organization may implement a policy that grants access to a confidential document only if the user has a security clearance level of "Top Secret," is using a company-issued device, and is connecting from an approved geographic region during business hours. This level of granularity would be difficult to achieve with traditional RBAC, which relies on static role assignments that do not consider contextual factors.

One of the primary advantages of ABAC is its ability to enforce the principle of least privilege in a more dynamic manner. Because access decisions are based on real-time attributes rather than predefined roles, users are granted only the permissions necessary for their specific situation. This reduces the risk of over-provisioned access, which is a common security issue in role-based systems. If a user's attributes change—such as a promotion to a new position or a shift in project assignments—their access rights automatically adjust without requiring manual intervention from administrators.

ABAC is also well-suited for environments that require fine-grained access control, such as government agencies, financial institutions, and healthcare organizations. Regulations such as the Health Insurance Portability and Accountability Act (HIPAA) and the General Data Protection Regulation (GDPR) impose strict requirements on how sensitive data is accessed and shared. ABAC enables organizations to define policies that enforce regulatory compliance by ensuring that only authorized individuals can access protected data under specific conditions. For instance, a policy might allow a nurse to view a patient's medical records only if they are currently assigned to that patient's care team, the access request originates from within the hospital network, and the request is made during a scheduled shift.

Despite its advantages, implementing ABAC comes with challenges. One of the most significant hurdles is the complexity of policy definition and management. Because ABAC relies on multiple attributes to make access decisions, organizations must establish and maintain a well-structured attribute management system. Defining policies requires a deep understanding of business processes, data classification, and user workflows. Organizations must also ensure that attributes remain accurate and up to date, as outdated or incorrect attributes can lead to unintended access grants or denials.

Another challenge is performance, particularly in large-scale environments with numerous users, resources, and attributes. ABAC requires evaluating multiple attributes in real time, which can increase the computational overhead of access requests. To mitigate this, organizations often implement caching mechanisms, policy optimization techniques, and efficient attribute retrieval methods. Advances in cloud computing and distributed architectures have also improved the scalability of ABAC, making it more practical for modern enterprises.

Integrating ABAC with existing identity and access management (IAM) solutions is another consideration for organizations looking to adopt this model. Many legacy systems are designed around RBAC, requiring modifications to support ABAC policies. Some organizations adopt a hybrid approach, combining RBAC and ABAC to leverage the strengths of both models. For example, an organization might use RBAC for general role-based access management while incorporating ABAC for more granular, context-aware controls. This approach allows for a gradual transition to ABAC without completely replacing existing role-based frameworks.

ABAC also plays a crucial role in Zero Trust security models, which assume that no entity should be trusted by default, even if it is inside the corporate network. In a Zero Trust environment, access decisions are continuously evaluated based on real-time attributes rather than static role memberships. ABAC enables organizations to implement dynamic policies that adapt to changing security conditions, such as detecting anomalies in user behavior or identifying unauthorized devices attempting to access sensitive data.

As artificial intelligence and machine learning continue to evolve, ABAC is expected to become even more intelligent and adaptive. AI-driven access control systems can analyze vast amounts of data to identify patterns, detect anomalies, and dynamically adjust policies based on risk assessments. For instance, if an AI system detects that a user is attempting to access sensitive files from an unusual location, it might trigger an additional authentication step or temporarily restrict access until further verification is performed.

Organizations implementing ABAC must invest in proper governance frameworks, attribute management strategies, and policy automation tools to ensure its effectiveness. While the initial setup may require significant effort, the long-term benefits of improved security, compliance, and flexibility make ABAC an attractive choice for modern access control needs. The ability to define policies based on a wide range of attributes allows organizations to tailor access control decisions to specific business requirements, reducing the risks associated with static and overly permissive access policies.

As IT environments continue to grow more complex and dynamic, ABAC provides a scalable and adaptive solution for managing access to critical resources. Its ability to incorporate real-time contextual factors into access decisions makes it a valuable tool for organizations seeking to enhance security while maintaining operational efficiency. By leveraging ABAC, businesses can achieve a higher level of precision in access control, reducing risks and ensuring that sensitive data remains protected under the right conditions.

Comparing RBAC and ABAC: Strengths and Weaknesses

Role-Based Access Control (RBAC) and Attribute-Based Access Control (ABAC) are two widely used models for managing access to systems and data. While both models serve the same fundamental purpose of restricting access to authorized users, they differ significantly in their approach, flexibility, and implementation complexity. Organizations must carefully evaluate the strengths and weaknesses of each model to determine which best suits their needs, or whether a hybrid approach may be necessary.

RBAC is based on predefined roles that determine a user's access rights within an organization. Users are assigned one or more roles, and each role is linked to a specific set of permissions. This model simplifies access control management by grouping users based on job functions rather than managing individual access permissions. The primary advantage of RBAC is its simplicity and ease of implementation. Once roles and associated permissions are established, managing access becomes straightforward, as administrators only need to assign or revoke roles rather than modifying permissions for each user.

RBAC is particularly effective in structured environments where job responsibilities are well-defined and do not frequently change. For example, in a corporate setting, an HR manager role can be configured with access to employee records, payroll information, and performance evaluations. When a new HR manager is hired, they are simply assigned the HR manager role, inheriting all relevant permissions without the need for manual configuration. This consistency improves security and reduces administrative overhead.

Another strength of RBAC is its ability to enforce the principle of least privilege by ensuring that users only receive the permissions associated with their roles. By carefully defining roles and avoiding excessive permissions, organizations can minimize the risk of unauthorized access. Additionally, RBAC supports regulatory compliance by providing a clear, auditable structure for managing access, making it easier to demonstrate compliance with standards such as HIPAA, GDPR, and SOX.

However, RBAC has its limitations. One of the most significant challenges is role explosion, which occurs when too many roles are created to accommodate different access needs. Over time, an organization may find itself managing hundreds or even thousands of roles, making administration complex and inefficient. As job functions evolve, existing roles may need frequent updates, leading to maintenance challenges. Additionally, RBAC struggles with dynamic access scenarios where permissions must change based on contextual factors such as time, location, or device type.

ABAC addresses many of the limitations of RBAC by introducing a more dynamic and fine-grained approach to access control. Instead of relying on static role assignments, ABAC evaluates multiple attributes related to users, resources, actions, and environmental conditions to determine access rights. Attributes can include factors such as job title, department, clearance level, geographic location, device security status, and time of access. This flexibility allows organizations to implement more precise access control policies that adapt to real-time conditions.

One of the primary advantages of ABAC is its ability to support complex and context-aware access control policies. For example, an ABAC policy could allow a financial analyst to access sensitive reports only during business hours from a corporate-managed device, but deny access if the request originates from an untrusted network. This level of granularity enhances security by considering multiple factors beyond just a user's role. ABAC is particularly beneficial in cloud-based and remote work environments, where users access resources from various devices and locations.

ABAC also improves scalability by eliminating the need for predefined roles. Instead of creating new roles for every unique combination of access requirements, organizations define policies based on attributes. This reduces administrative burden and prevents role explosion. Because ABAC policies are rule-based and not tied to static roles, they can be easily updated without requiring significant restructuring of the access control framework.

Despite its strengths, ABAC is not without challenges. One of the biggest hurdles in implementing ABAC is its complexity. Defining attribute-based policies requires a thorough understanding of business processes, security requirements, and contextual factors that influence access decisions. Unlike RBAC, where roles and permissions are relatively easy to define, ABAC policies must account for a potentially vast number of attributes and their interdependencies. This complexity can make policy management difficult, requiring specialized tools and expertise.

Performance is another consideration when deploying ABAC. Because access decisions involve evaluating multiple attributes in real-time, ABAC can introduce computational overhead, particularly in large-scale environments with high transaction volumes. Organizations must implement efficient attribute management and policy evaluation mechanisms to prevent performance bottlenecks. Additionally, maintaining accurate attribute data is critical, as outdated or incorrect attributes could lead to unintended access grants or denials.

Another challenge with ABAC is adoption. Many organizations already have well-established RBAC systems, making it difficult to transition entirely to ABAC. In such cases, a hybrid approach that combines RBAC and ABAC may be more practical. For example, an organization can use RBAC to manage baseline access rights and then layer ABAC policies on top to introduce dynamic, context-aware restrictions. This approach allows organizations to leverage the strengths of both models while minimizing the challenges associated with each.

Ultimately, the choice between RBAC and ABAC depends on an organization's security requirements, operational complexity, and resource availability. RBAC is well-suited for environments with stable job functions and regulatory compliance needs, while ABAC provides greater flexibility for dynamic and high-security environments. Many organizations find that a combination of both models offers the best balance between manageability and adaptability, ensuring that access control remains effective as business and technology landscapes continue to evolve.

The Principle of Least Privilege (PoLP)

The Principle of Least Privilege (PoLP) is a fundamental security concept that dictates that users, applications, and systems should be granted only the minimum access necessary to perform their required tasks. By restricting privileges to the bare minimum, organizations can reduce the risk of unauthorized access, data breaches, and insider threats. This principle applies to all aspects of cybersecurity, including user permissions, network access, system configurations, and software execution.

The primary goal of PoLP is to minimize the attack surface of an organization by limiting unnecessary access rights. When users or applications have more privileges than required, they pose a greater security risk. A compromised account with excessive privileges can lead to data leaks, privilege escalation attacks, or the spread of malware. By enforcing PoLP, organizations ensure that even if an account or system is compromised, the potential damage remains limited.

In traditional access control models, it is common for employees to be granted more access than they actually need, either due to convenience or administrative oversight. Over time, users may accumulate excessive permissions as they take on new roles or work on different projects. This accumulation of privileges, often referred to as "privilege creep," increases security risks and makes it harder to enforce proper access controls. Regular audits and role reviews help prevent privilege creep and ensure that users retain only the permissions necessary for their current responsibilities.

One of the most critical areas where PoLP is applied is user account management. In most organizations, employees are divided into different roles based on their job functions. A well-implemented PoLP strategy ensures that an employee in the marketing department, for example, does not have access to financial records or system configuration settings. Administrative privileges should be reserved for IT staff responsible for system maintenance, and even within IT teams, access should be segmented based on specific responsibilities.

Privileged accounts, such as administrator and root accounts, require special attention in PoLP enforcement. These accounts have unrestricted access to critical systems and are prime targets for cyberattacks. Organizations should adopt the principle of least privilege by limiting the use of privileged accounts and implementing just-in-time (JIT) access mechanisms. JIT access allows users to obtain elevated privileges only when needed and only for a limited time, reducing the risk of misuse.

The concept of PoLP also extends beyond human users to applications and system processes. Many software applications and services require access to databases, files, and network resources to function properly. However, granting applications excessive permissions can lead to security vulnerabilities. For instance, a web application that only needs read access to a database should not be given write or delete privileges. If the application is compromised, an attacker would be limited in what they could do. Similarly, system processes and scripts should run with the lowest possible privileges to prevent unauthorized actions in the event of an exploit.

Operating systems and security frameworks provide various mechanisms to enforce PoLP. Modern operating systems support role-based access control (RBAC), attribute-based access control (ABAC), and mandatory access control (MAC), all of which help define and restrict permissions based on user roles, attributes, or predefined security policies. File system permissions, user access controls, and least-privilege execution settings further ensure that applications and users do not exceed their necessary privileges.

Network security also benefits from PoLP by restricting access to sensitive resources. Firewalls, network segmentation, and zero trust architectures use the principle of least privilege to limit traffic between systems. For example, a database server should not be directly accessible from the internet, and only specific application servers should be allowed to communicate with it. By enforcing strict network access controls, organizations can reduce the likelihood of unauthorized access and lateral movement within their infrastructure.

PoLP plays a crucial role in cloud security, where access control must be carefully managed across distributed environments. Cloud platforms provide fine-grained access control mechanisms such as identity and access management (IAM) policies, service roles, and least-privilege access configurations. Organizations using cloud services must ensure that accounts, applications, and virtual machines are provisioned with only the permissions necessary to perform their intended functions. Overly permissive configurations, such as granting broad administrative privileges to cloud resources, can lead to serious security breaches if exploited.

One of the biggest challenges in implementing PoLP is balancing security with usability. Restricting access too much can create operational inefficiencies, causing frustration among employees who require legitimate access to perform their work. This challenge can be addressed by implementing role-based access models, automating access request workflows, and providing temporary elevated privileges when necessary. Organizations should also educate employees on the importance of PoLP to ensure compliance and reduce resistance to security measures.

Security frameworks and regulatory standards often mandate the enforcement of PoLP as part of best practices. Regulations such as the General Data Protection Regulation (GDPR), the Health Insurance Portability and Accountability Act (HIPAA), and the Payment Card Industry Data Security Standard (PCI DSS) require organizations to implement access controls that limit data exposure to authorized individuals. Demonstrating compliance with these regulations often involves documenting access policies, conducting regular privilege audits, and implementing technical controls to enforce PoLP.

Automation and artificial intelligence (AI) are increasingly being used to improve PoLP enforcement. Automated identity and access management (IAM) systems can continuously monitor and adjust permissions based on user behavior and risk analysis. AI-driven security solutions can detect anomalies, such as a user accessing a system they do not normally use, and trigger security responses such as revoking access or requiring additional authentication. By integrating automation with PoLP principles, organizations can enhance security while reducing the administrative burden of manually managing access rights.

Regular reviews and audits are essential to maintaining PoLP over time. Organizations should conduct periodic access reviews to identify unnecessary privileges, revoke outdated permissions, and ensure that users and applications are following least-privilege principles. Continuous monitoring tools help detect privilege escalations and policy violations, allowing security teams to respond quickly to potential threats.

By enforcing PoLP across all aspects of IT security, organizations can significantly reduce their risk exposure while maintaining operational efficiency. Least privilege ensures that access is granted only when necessary and only to those who require it, minimizing the potential damage of security breaches and insider threats. With proper implementation, automation, and continuous monitoring, PoLP remains one of the most effective strategies for strengthening cybersecurity in any environment.

Separation of Duties (SoD) in Access Control

Separation of Duties (SoD) is a fundamental principle in access control and security that aims to reduce the risk of fraud, errors, and abuse by dividing critical tasks among multiple individuals. By ensuring that no single person has complete control over a sensitive process, organizations can prevent unauthorized actions, detect suspicious activities, and maintain the integrity of their operations. SoD is particularly important in industries where financial transactions, regulatory compliance, and data protection are critical, such as banking, healthcare, and government.

The primary objective of SoD is to create a system of checks and balances that limits the power and influence of any one individual over key business functions. Without SoD, an employee with excessive privileges could manipulate systems, commit fraud, or cause unintentional harm without oversight. By requiring multiple individuals to participate in sensitive processes, organizations introduce accountability and reduce the likelihood of malicious activity going undetected.

A common example of SoD is in financial transactions, where the person who authorizes a payment should not be the same person who processes or approves it. If a single employee has the ability to both request and approve payments, there is a high risk of fraudulent transactions. By separating these duties, organizations ensure that no individual can execute unauthorized payments without detection. This concept is also widely applied in auditing, where the person responsible for recording transactions should not be the same individual who reviews financial statements.

In information security, SoD is used to prevent privilege abuse and unauthorized access to sensitive systems. For example, a system administrator who manages user accounts should not have the ability to approve security policy changes without review. Similarly, software developers who write code should not be the ones to approve or deploy it into production without an independent review process. By enforcing SoD in IT environments, organizations can minimize insider threats, reduce human errors, and ensure that security policies are consistently followed.

SoD is closely linked to the Principle of Least Privilege (PoLP), which ensures that users are granted only the minimum permissions necessary to perform their job functions. While PoLP limits excessive access, SoD takes it a step further by requiring that critical tasks be divided among multiple users. This dual-layered approach significantly strengthens security by making it more difficult for any one individual to bypass security controls.

Implementing SoD in access control requires careful planning and role design. Organizations must analyze their business processes to identify tasks that require separation and determine which roles should be assigned to different individuals. Role-Based Access Control (RBAC) is often used to enforce SoD by defining roles with distinct responsibilities and ensuring that conflicting duties are assigned to separate users. For instance, in an ERP system, a role that allows a user to create vendor invoices should not be combined with a role that approves payments.

One challenge in implementing SoD is balancing security with operational efficiency. In smaller organizations with limited personnel, enforcing strict SoD policies may be impractical, as employees often wear multiple hats. In such cases, organizations may use alternative controls such as automated transaction monitoring, supervisor approvals, and audit logs to compensate for the lack of personnel to separate duties. Automated workflows and approval mechanisms can help enforce SoD without introducing excessive administrative overhead.

Another challenge is managing SoD in dynamic environments where employees' responsibilities frequently change. Organizations must regularly review and update access control policies to ensure that users do not accumulate conflicting permissions over time. Privilege creep, where employees retain access rights from previous roles, can lead to SoD violations if left unchecked. Conducting periodic access reviews and using identity governance solutions can help organizations identify and remediate SoD conflicts.

SoD is also a key requirement in regulatory compliance frameworks such as the Sarbanes-Oxley Act (SOX), the Health Insurance Portability and Accountability Act (HIPAA), and the Payment Card Industry Data Security Standard (PCI DSS). These regulations mandate that organizations implement controls to prevent fraud, data breaches, and unauthorized access to financial or personal information. Auditors often review SoD policies to ensure that organizations have adequate controls in place to mitigate security risks.

To effectively enforce SoD, organizations can implement preventive, detective, and corrective controls. Preventive controls, such as access control policies and automated workflows, restrict users from performing conflicting tasks in the first place. Detective controls, such as audit logs and anomaly detection systems, help identify violations of SoD policies after they occur. Corrective controls, such as periodic access reviews and policy updates, help organizations continuously refine and enforce SoD policies.

Technology plays a crucial role in automating SoD enforcement. Identity and Access Management (IAM) solutions, Privileged Access Management (PAM) tools, and Governance, Risk, and Compliance (GRC) platforms enable organizations to define, monitor, and enforce SoD policies at scale. These systems can automatically flag conflicts, enforce approval workflows, and provide detailed audit trails to support compliance efforts.

In cloud-based environments, enforcing SoD becomes more complex as access is often distributed across multiple platforms and services. Cloud providers offer IAM controls that allow organizations to define granular access policies and enforce least-privilege principles. However, cloud environments require continuous monitoring to detect SoD violations, as users may gain unauthorized access through misconfigured permissions, API integrations, or shadow IT. Implementing cloud security posture management (CSPM) solutions can help organizations maintain visibility and enforce SoD policies across distributed environments.

Enforcing SoD is not just a technical challenge but also a cultural and organizational one. Employees must understand the importance of access controls and the risks associated with excessive privileges.

Security awareness training can help employees recognize the need for SoD and encourage them to follow security best practices. Additionally, management must be committed to enforcing access control policies and ensuring that security is not compromised for the sake of convenience.

Organizations that successfully implement SoD benefit from increased security, reduced fraud risk, and improved compliance with regulatory requirements. While implementing SoD may require careful planning and continuous oversight, it is a critical component of a strong access control strategy. By systematically dividing responsibilities, enforcing access restrictions, and leveraging technology to automate controls, organizations can build a resilient security framework that protects their systems, data, and business processes from threats.

Access Control Policies: Design and Implementation

Access control policies define the rules and conditions under which users, applications, and systems can access resources. These policies are the backbone of security frameworks, ensuring that only authorized individuals or processes can interact with sensitive data and systems. Effective access control policies must balance security, usability, and compliance, adapting to an organization's evolving needs while minimizing the risk of unauthorized access. The design and implementation of access control policies require careful planning, alignment with business objectives, and ongoing monitoring to maintain effectiveness.

The foundation of access control policies is determining who should have access to what resources and under what conditions. This involves defining access levels, setting authorization rules, and ensuring that security requirements align with organizational roles and responsibilities. Policies should be based on key principles such as the Principle of Least Privilege (PoLP), which ensures that users only receive the minimum permissions necessary to perform their tasks, and Separation of Duties (SoD), which prevents conflicts of interest by dividing critical tasks among multiple individuals.

Organizations must first assess their security requirements before designing access control policies. This involves identifying sensitive assets, classifying data based on confidentiality and importance, and understanding who needs access to these resources. A comprehensive risk assessment helps define the scope of access control policies, ensuring that security measures are proportionate to the value of the protected information. For instance, highly sensitive financial data may require stricter access controls compared to general internal documents.

There are several access control models that organizations can use to structure their policies. Discretionary Access Control (DAC) allows resource owners to define access permissions, providing flexibility but also increasing the risk of misconfigurations. Mandatory Access Control (MAC) enforces strict policies based on security classifications, commonly used in government and military environments. Role-Based Access Control (RBAC) assigns permissions based on predefined roles within the organization, simplifying access management for structured environments. Attribute-Based Access Control (ABAC) offers a more dynamic approach by evaluating multiple attributes, such as user roles, device security posture, and contextual factors like time and location, before granting access. Organizations often use a combination of these models to achieve a balance between flexibility and security.

The implementation of access control policies requires a structured approach that includes defining policies, integrating them into systems, enforcing compliance, and continuously monitoring effectiveness. Policies should be documented in a clear and standardized format, outlining access requirements, approval workflows, and exception handling procedures. Organizations should also establish governance mechanisms to review and update policies regularly to reflect changes in business operations, regulatory requirements, and emerging security threats.

Once policies are defined, they must be enforced through technical controls. Identity and Access Management (IAM) systems play a critical role in managing access control policies by centralizing authentication, authorization, and user identity verification. IAM solutions can integrate with directory services, single sign-on (SSO) mechanisms, and multi-factor authentication (MFA) to strengthen security. Access control policies must also be implemented within applications, databases, and network security devices such as firewalls and intrusion prevention systems.

Access control policies should be configured with granularity to minimize the risk of over-permissioned accounts. Overly broad permissions increase the attack surface and make it easier for attackers to exploit unauthorized access. For example, instead of granting all employees access to a shared drive, policies should define access based on job roles, departments, and data sensitivity. Fine-grained access control ensures that users can only access the specific resources they need for their work.

Automation plays an important role in enforcing access control policies and reducing administrative overhead. Automated provisioning and de-provisioning ensure that users receive appropriate access when they join an organization and that their access is revoked when they leave. Role mining and machine learning techniques can help identify redundant or unnecessary permissions, optimizing access control configurations. Policy-based automation also enables real-time decision-making based on risk assessments, such as restricting access to critical systems if a user logs in from an unfamiliar location or device.

Access reviews and audits are essential to maintaining the integrity of access control policies. Periodic reviews help organizations identify policy violations, detect privilege creep, and ensure compliance with security frameworks such as ISO 27001, NIST, and regulatory requirements like GDPR and HIPAA. Audit logs provide visibility into access requests, approvals, and denials, enabling security teams to investigate incidents and detect unauthorized activity.

Organizations must also consider how access control policies apply in cloud environments. As businesses increasingly migrate to cloud-based infrastructures, enforcing consistent access control policies across on-premises and cloud systems becomes a challenge. Cloud service providers offer built-in IAM solutions, but organizations must ensure that policies are properly configured to prevent misconfigurations that could expose sensitive data. Cloud access security brokers (CASBs) and zero trust security models help extend access control policies to distributed and hybrid environments.

User education and awareness are critical to the successful implementation of access control policies. Employees should understand the importance of access controls, follow best practices for handling credentials, and report suspicious activities. Social engineering attacks, such as phishing, often target employees to gain unauthorized access, making it essential for organizations to implement security awareness training alongside technical access control measures.

Incident response planning should also be integrated with access control policies. In the event of a security breach or policy violation, organizations must have predefined procedures to revoke access, isolate affected systems, and investigate the root cause of the incident. A well-prepared response plan ensures that access control mechanisms are reinforced in the wake of security incidents, reducing the likelihood of recurring threats.

A well-designed access control policy framework enables organizations to protect sensitive data, enforce regulatory compliance, and minimize security risks. By implementing policies that align with business needs and leveraging automation for enforcement, organizations can maintain a robust access control posture. Continuous monitoring, regular audits, and adaptive security measures ensure that access control policies remain effective in an ever-changing security landscape.

Identity, Authentication, and Authorization

Identity, authentication, and authorization are the three fundamental pillars of access control and cybersecurity. These concepts work together to ensure that only legitimate users and systems can access resources while preventing unauthorized access. Understanding the differences between identity, authentication, and authorization is crucial for designing and implementing secure access control mechanisms in modern IT environments.

Identity serves as the foundation of access control. It represents a unique entity, whether a person, a device, an application, or a service. In a digital context, an identity is typically associated with a username, email address, or unique identifier stored in an identity management system. Every user or system that interacts with a network, application, or database must have a distinct identity to differentiate it from others. Identity management involves creating, maintaining, and revoking identities as necessary, ensuring that each entity is accurately represented within an organization's security infrastructure.

Authentication is the process of verifying that an entity is who it claims to be. Simply having an identity is not enough; authentication ensures that the user or system providing the identity has legitimate ownership of it. Traditional authentication methods rely on passwords, which have long been the standard for verifying identities. However, passwords come with significant security risks, including weak credentials, reuse across multiple accounts, and vulnerability to phishing attacks.

To enhance security, organizations increasingly rely on multi-factor authentication (MFA). MFA requires users to provide two or more forms of verification, typically categorized into three factors: something they know (a password or PIN), something they have (a security token or mobile device), and something they are (biometric data such as fingerprints or facial recognition). By requiring multiple authentication factors, MFA reduces the risk of unauthorized access, even if one factor is compromised.

Modern authentication mechanisms also leverage passwordless authentication methods to enhance security and usability. These methods use biometrics, smart cards, or cryptographic keys to authenticate users without requiring traditional passwords. Single Sign-On (SSO) is another authentication approach that simplifies access by allowing users to log in once and gain access to multiple applications without repeatedly entering credentials. SSO improves user experience while reducing the likelihood of password-related security breaches.

Once authentication is successfully completed, the next step is authorization. While authentication verifies identity, authorization determines what actions the authenticated user or system is permitted to perform. Authorization is enforced through access control policies that define permissions based on various criteria, such as user roles, attributes, and security policies.

Role-Based Access Control (RBAC) is a widely used authorization model that assigns permissions based on predefined roles within an organization. Under RBAC, users are granted access rights according to their job functions, ensuring that they can only perform actions necessary for their responsibilities. For example, an HR employee may have permission to access payroll records but not IT system configurations. RBAC simplifies access management by grouping users into roles rather than managing individual permissions.

Attribute-Based Access Control (ABAC) extends RBAC by incorporating additional contextual factors such as time of access, location, device security posture, and user attributes. ABAC allows for more dynamic and fine-grained authorization decisions. For example, an organization may implement a policy that allows employees to access sensitive data only from company-approved devices during business hours. This level of flexibility enhances security by adapting to changing conditions while still enforcing strict access control policies.

Access control mechanisms must integrate identity, authentication, and authorization to create a seamless security framework. Identity and Access Management (IAM) solutions play a critical role in managing user identities, enforcing authentication policies, and defining authorization rules. IAM systems centralize identity management, automate user provisioning and de-provisioning, and ensure consistent enforcement of access policies across an organization's IT infrastructure.

The emergence of Zero Trust security models has reshaped traditional authentication and authorization approaches. Zero Trust operates on the principle that no entity should be automatically trusted, even if it is inside the corporate network. Instead of granting broad access based on initial authentication, Zero Trust continuously evaluates trust levels by considering real-time factors such as user behavior, device security, and risk assessments. This approach minimizes the risk of unauthorized access by ensuring that authentication and authorization are enforced dynamically throughout a user's session.

Identity verification and authentication extend beyond human users. In modern IT environments, applications, services, and Internet of

Things (IoT) devices also require authentication to communicate securely. Machine identities, including API keys, digital certificates, and cryptographic tokens, help establish trust between systems. Managing these non-human identities is essential to securing cloud environments, microservices architectures, and automated workflows.

The security of identity, authentication, and authorization mechanisms depends on continuous monitoring and risk assessment. Organizations must implement logging and auditing to track authentication attempts, authorization decisions, and policy violations. Security Information and Event Management (SIEM) solutions analyze authentication data to detect anomalies, such as repeated failed login attempts or unauthorized access attempts from unusual locations. By leveraging threat intelligence and behavioral analytics, organizations can proactively respond to security threats and mitigate identity-based attacks.

Regulatory compliance also plays a significant role in shaping identity and access control strategies. Many industries must adhere to strict regulations such as the General Data Protection Regulation (GDPR), the Health Insurance Portability and Accountability Act (HIPAA), and the Payment Card Industry Data Security Standard (PCI DSS). These regulations require organizations to implement strong authentication mechanisms, restrict access to sensitive data, and maintain detailed audit logs of identity-related activities. Failure to comply with these requirements can result in legal penalties, financial losses, and reputational damage.

As organizations adopt cloud computing, remote work, and digital transformation initiatives, the need for robust identity, authentication, and authorization strategies becomes even more critical. Cloud environments require federated identity management, enabling users to authenticate across multiple cloud services using a unified identity. Identity federation simplifies access while ensuring consistent enforcement of security policies across hybrid and multi-cloud environments.

Artificial intelligence and machine learning are increasingly being integrated into identity and authentication processes. AI-driven authentication solutions analyze behavioral patterns to detect anomalies and adjust authentication requirements dynamically. For example, if a user logs in from an unusual location, the system may prompt for additional verification before granting access. Machine learning models enhance security by identifying suspicious activities that traditional authentication methods might overlook.

Identity, authentication, and authorization are essential components of a comprehensive security framework. By implementing strong identity management practices, enforcing robust authentication mechanisms, and applying dynamic authorization policies, organizations can protect their systems and data from unauthorized access. As cyber threats continue to evolve, businesses must stay ahead by adopting innovative authentication technologies, refining access control policies, and continuously monitoring identity-related security risks.

The Role of Policy Enforcement Points (PEP) and Policy Decision Points (PDP)

In modern access control systems, security policies must be enforced dynamically and consistently across an organization's infrastructure. Two critical components that enable this are the Policy Enforcement Point (PEP) and the Policy Decision Point (PDP). These elements work together to ensure that access control policies are applied in real time, based on predefined rules and contextual information. Understanding the roles of PEP and PDP is essential for designing robust access control architectures that support Role-Based Access Control (RBAC), Attribute-Based Access Control (ABAC), and Zero Trust security models.

The Policy Enforcement Point (PEP) is responsible for enforcing access control decisions at the point of resource access. Whenever a user, application, or system attempts to access a protected resource, the request is intercepted by the PEP. The PEP does not make decisions on whether access should be granted or denied; rather, it acts as a gatekeeper, forwarding access requests to the Policy Decision Point (PDP) for evaluation. Once the PDP returns a decision, the PEP enforces the outcome by allowing or denying access based on the policy rules.

PEPs exist at various layers of an IT environment. They can be implemented in network security devices such as firewalls, VPN gateways, and intrusion prevention systems to control access at the network level. In application security, PEPs are embedded within authentication and authorization mechanisms, such as identity providers and single sign-on (SSO) solutions. At the operating system level, PEPs are responsible for managing file permissions, system processes, and API access controls. Regardless of their placement, all PEPs share the fundamental role of intercepting access requests and ensuring compliance with security policies.

The Policy Decision Point (PDP) is the component responsible for evaluating access requests and making policy-based decisions. When a request reaches the PEP, it is forwarded to the PDP, which analyzes the request against predefined policies to determine whether access should be granted. The PDP evaluates multiple factors, including the identity of the requester, the sensitivity of the resource, environmental conditions such as location and time, and risk assessments based on behavioral analysis. Once the decision is made, the PDP returns the result to the PEP for enforcement.

The PDP operates using a policy engine that processes rules written in a standardized access control language. Many organizations use eXtensible Access Control Markup Language (XACML) to define their access policies, allowing for flexible and granular decision-making. XACML enables administrators to specify complex access control conditions, such as allowing access only if a user is part of a specific department, using an approved device, and connecting from an authorized location. By leveraging standardized policy languages, PDPs provide organizations with a scalable way to manage access control decisions across distributed environments.

One of the key advantages of separating policy enforcement and policy decision-making is scalability. In large enterprise environments, a single centralized PDP can handle policy evaluations for multiple PEPs deployed across different systems and networks. This separation reduces the complexity of managing access control at individual enforcement points while ensuring consistent application of policies across the organization. Furthermore, by centralizing policy decisions, organizations can streamline compliance audits and reduce the risk of inconsistent access control configurations.

PEPs and PDPs are fundamental components of Attribute-Based Access Control (ABAC) systems, where access decisions are based on a combination of attributes rather than static role assignments. In an ABAC implementation, the PDP evaluates attributes such as user role, department, security clearance, device type, and location to determine whether access should be granted. The PEP ensures that access is granted or denied according to the decision made by the PDP, ensuring enforcement at the resource level. This model allows organizations to implement more dynamic and context-aware access control policies.

The role of PEPs and PDPs is also critical in Zero Trust security architectures, where no entity is automatically trusted, and access must be continuously verified. In a Zero Trust environment, every access request is evaluated based on contextual factors, and decisions are made dynamically. The PDP assesses real-time risk signals, such as user behavior anomalies, device posture, and geographic access patterns, to determine whether a request should be approved. The PEP enforces the decision, allowing or blocking access based on the PDP's risk evaluation. By continuously evaluating access requests, organizations can minimize the risk of insider threats and credential-based attacks.

Cloud computing and hybrid IT environments have further increased the importance of PEPs and PDPs. In cloud-based infrastructure, access control policies must be enforced across multiple platforms, including on-premises data centers, public cloud services, and SaaS applications. Cloud-native PDPs integrate with Identity and Access Management (IAM) solutions, allowing organizations to define policies that span multiple cloud providers. PEPs deployed in cloud environments enforce access decisions at the API, container, and microservices levels, ensuring secure access to distributed applications and data.

The performance of access control systems depends on the efficiency of PEP and PDP interactions. If the PDP introduces latency due to complex policy evaluations, access requests may be delayed, impacting user experience. To mitigate performance issues, organizations implement caching mechanisms at the PEP level, storing previously approved access decisions for a defined period. Additionally, PDPs can be distributed across multiple data centers to handle high volumes of access requests with minimal latency. By optimizing the interaction between PEPs and PDPs, organizations can maintain a balance between security and performance.

To enhance the security and reliability of PEPs and PDPs, organizations must implement robust monitoring and auditing mechanisms. Logs generated by PEPs provide visibility into access attempts, policy violations, and denied requests, allowing security teams to detect anomalies and potential security incidents. PDP logs track policy evaluations, decision rationales, and attribute usage, enabling organizations to audit policy effectiveness and ensure compliance with regulatory requirements. By analyzing PEP and PDP logs, organizations can improve their access control strategies and detect emerging threats.

The evolution of access control has led to the integration of artificial intelligence (AI) and machine learning (ML) in policy decision-making. AI-enhanced PDPs can analyze historical access patterns and detect anomalies that indicate potential security threats. For example, if an employee who typically logs in from an office location suddenly attempts to access a critical system from an unfamiliar country, the PDP can trigger additional authentication measures before granting access. By incorporating AI-driven risk analysis, organizations can make more intelligent and adaptive access control decisions.

PEPs and PDPs are essential for enforcing modern access control policies, ensuring that access decisions are applied consistently across an organization's IT infrastructure. The separation of policy enforcement and policy decision-making enables scalability, flexibility, and enhanced security. As organizations continue to adopt Zero Trust architectures, cloud-based environments, and AI-driven security models, the role of PEPs and PDPs will remain central to safeguarding critical systems and data. Implementing efficient and well-integrated policy enforcement and decision-making mechanisms is crucial for maintaining strong access control frameworks in an increasingly complex cybersecurity landscape.

Core Components of RBAC

Role-Based Access Control (RBAC) is a widely adopted access control model that provides organizations with a structured and scalable way to manage permissions. By assigning users to roles rather than granting permissions directly, RBAC simplifies administrative overhead, improves security, and ensures that users have only the necessary level of access to perform their tasks. The core components of RBAC define how access is structured and managed within an organization, ensuring that permissions are assigned, enforced, and reviewed systematically.

The foundation of RBAC is built upon three primary elements: users, roles, and permissions. Users represent individuals, applications, or systems that require access to resources. Each user is assigned to one or more roles, which define the specific permissions they inherit. Permissions represent the actions that a role can perform on a resource, such as reading a document, modifying a database, or executing a system command. This three-tiered structure ensures that access control remains consistent and manageable, reducing the risk of privilege misconfigurations and unauthorized access.

Roles are the central component of RBAC, serving as an abstraction layer between users and permissions. A role is typically designed to reflect a job function, department, or organizational responsibility. For example, an organization may define roles such as "HR Manager," "Finance Analyst," or "IT Administrator," each with a specific set of permissions aligned with their respective job functions. Users are then assigned roles based on their responsibilities, ensuring that they receive the appropriate level of access without the need for direct permission assignments.

A key feature of RBAC is role hierarchy, which allows roles to inherit permissions from other roles. This hierarchical structure simplifies role management by enabling higher-level roles to automatically include the permissions of lower-level roles. For example, a "Senior Developer" role may inherit all the permissions of a "Developer" role while adding additional privileges, such as approving code changes. Role hierarchies help organizations reduce redundancy, maintain consistency, and streamline access control administration.

Separation of Duties (SoD) is another critical component of RBAC, ensuring that conflicting permissions are not assigned to the same user. SoD prevents users from having excessive control over critical processes, reducing the risk of fraud, errors, or security breaches. For example, in a financial system, the role responsible for initiating payments should not be able to approve them. By enforcing SoD policies, organizations can mitigate insider threats and maintain regulatory compliance.

RBAC also supports constraints, which impose additional rules on role assignments and permission usage. Constraints can be used to enforce policies such as limiting the number of users assigned to a specific role, restricting access based on time or location, or requiring multi-party approval before granting certain privileges. These constraints provide organizations with greater flexibility in defining access control policies while ensuring that security requirements are met.

Role engineering is the process of designing and defining roles within an organization. Effective role engineering requires a thorough understanding of business processes, job functions, and security requirements. Organizations must carefully analyze user access needs to create well-structured roles that minimize the risk of role explosion—an issue where too many roles are created, leading to administrative complexity. Role mining techniques, which analyze existing access patterns, can help identify optimal role definitions and reduce redundancy.

User-role assignment is another essential component of RBAC. Users can be assigned to roles manually by administrators or automatically based on predefined rules. Automated role assignment is particularly useful in large organizations where managing individual user access manually would be inefficient. Identity and Access Management (IAM) solutions often integrate with RBAC to automate role provisioning and de-provisioning based on employee onboarding, promotions, or terminations.

Permission-role mapping defines which permissions are associated with each role. This mapping ensures that roles align with business functions and security policies. Organizations must carefully design permission assignments to prevent excessive privileges and reduce the risk of privilege escalation attacks. Regular access reviews help validate that roles and permissions remain appropriate over time, adjusting as necessary to reflect organizational changes.

RBAC implementations often include session management, allowing users to activate only specific roles during a session rather than having all assigned roles active at once. This feature is particularly useful in environments where users have multiple roles with varying levels of access. By enabling users to switch roles dynamically, organizations can enforce stricter access control policies while maintaining operational flexibility.

Auditing and compliance play a significant role in RBAC by ensuring that access policies are followed and that unauthorized privilege escalations do not occur. Many regulatory frameworks, such as GDPR, HIPAA, and SOX, require organizations to maintain detailed logs of access activities. RBAC facilitates compliance by providing a structured and auditable access control model that aligns with security best practices.

RBAC is also highly adaptable to cloud and hybrid environments, where access control must be enforced across multiple platforms. Cloud service providers offer RBAC capabilities that integrate with enterprise IAM solutions, enabling organizations to manage access across on-premises and cloud-based systems. As organizations adopt Zero Trust security models, RBAC remains a fundamental component in ensuring that users receive only the necessary permissions to perform their duties.

To enhance RBAC's effectiveness, organizations must continuously evaluate and refine their role structures, permissions, and policies. Regular role reviews, automated policy enforcement, and integration with advanced security frameworks help organizations maintain a robust access control system. By leveraging the core components of RBAC, organizations can achieve a balance between security, operational efficiency, and regulatory compliance while minimizing access-related risks.

Role Hierarchies and Inheritance

Role hierarchies and inheritance are fundamental concepts in Role-Based Access Control (RBAC), providing a structured way to manage and assign permissions efficiently. These mechanisms allow roles to be organized in a hierarchical structure where higher-level roles inherit permissions from lower-level roles. By implementing role hierarchies, organizations can simplify role management, reduce redundancy, and maintain a consistent access control framework that aligns with business operations.

The primary purpose of role hierarchies is to establish relationships between different roles based on their level of authority and responsibility. In a hierarchical RBAC model, roles are structured in a way that allows senior roles to automatically acquire the permissions of their subordinate roles. This inheritance mechanism eliminates the need to manually assign redundant permissions to multiple roles, streamlining administrative efforts and ensuring a clear separation of duties. For example, if an organization defines a role structure where a "Manager" role inherits permissions from an "Employee" role, then all users assigned the "Manager" role automatically have access to the same resources as regular employees, along with additional privileges specific to managerial responsibilities.

Role inheritance reduces complexity by grouping related permissions into structured layers. Instead of defining permissions for each role separately, administrators can establish role relationships that naturally propagate permissions upward in the hierarchy. This approach not only simplifies role assignment but also improves security by ensuring that access rights are distributed consistently across the organization. If changes need to be made, administrators can modify a single role in the hierarchy, and those changes will be inherited by all related roles, reducing the risk of misconfigurations and access inconsistencies.

An essential aspect of role hierarchies is defining the scope of inheritance. Not all inherited permissions should be granted blindly; organizations must establish rules that determine which permissions should be passed along and which should be restricted. In some cases, role hierarchies may include constraints that prevent certain permissions from propagating to higher-level roles. This is particularly useful in enforcing Separation of Duties (SoD), where conflicting access rights should not be combined within a single role. For example, in a financial system, a role responsible for approving transactions should not inherit permissions from a role responsible for processing payments.

Organizations typically define role hierarchies based on job functions, business units, or levels of authority. A well-structured hierarchy reflects the organization's operational structure, ensuring that employees receive access relevant to their job responsibilities. A typical role hierarchy might include entry-level roles at the bottom, mid-level roles in the middle, and executive roles at the top. Each higher-tier role automatically inherits permissions from the lower-tier roles beneath it, maintaining a logical and scalable access control structure.

Role hierarchies also improve onboarding and offboarding processes. When a new employee joins an organization, they are assigned a role based on their job function, and their access permissions are automatically inherited from the appropriate role hierarchy. Similarly, if an employee is promoted or moves to a different department, their access rights can be adjusted by reassigning their role within the hierarchy, rather than manually modifying individual permissions. This reduces administrative overhead and ensures that employees receive appropriate access without delays.

Another benefit of role inheritance is its ability to enhance compliance and auditability. Many regulatory frameworks require organizations to enforce strict access control policies and maintain clear records of permission assignments. By using role hierarchies, organizations can demonstrate that access control policies are applied consistently and that no unauthorized privileges are granted outside the defined structure. Auditors can review the role hierarchy to verify that users have access only to the resources necessary for their job functions, reducing the risk of privilege abuse and security breaches.

However, while role hierarchies provide significant advantages, they also introduce challenges that must be carefully managed. One potential issue is role explosion, where an excessive number of roles are created to accommodate different levels of access. If hierarchies become too complex, managing them can become difficult, leading to administrative inefficiencies and potential security gaps. To prevent role explosion, organizations should carefully design role structures, consolidate redundant roles, and regularly review role definitions to ensure they remain relevant.

Another challenge is preventing unnecessary privilege escalation through poorly designed hierarchies. If a role inherits permissions that exceed what is necessary for its function, it could create security vulnerabilities. Organizations must conduct regular role audits and apply the Principle of Least Privilege (PoLP) to ensure that inherited permissions align with actual job responsibilities. Role constraints, such as limiting inheritance to specific categories of permissions, can help mitigate this risk.

Organizations implementing role hierarchies should also consider integrating automation tools to streamline role management. Identity and Access Management (IAM) solutions, Privileged Access Management (PAM) tools, and governance frameworks can help automate role assignments, track inheritance relationships, and enforce policy-based constraints. Automated role management reduces the risk of human error and ensures that role hierarchies remain consistent as the organization evolves.

Role hierarchies and inheritance play a crucial role in ensuring scalable, efficient, and secure access control within an organization. By leveraging these concepts, businesses can simplify permission management, improve security posture, and maintain compliance with industry regulations. A well-designed role hierarchy allows organizations to enforce structured access control policies, reducing administrative burden while maintaining flexibility in managing user privileges. Through careful planning, continuous monitoring, and the use of automation tools, organizations can effectively implement role hierarchies that align with their security and operational needs.

Role Engineering: Best Practices

Role engineering is the process of defining, designing, and managing roles in a Role-Based Access Control (RBAC) system to ensure that access rights align with business needs while maintaining security and efficiency. Well-structured roles simplify access management, improve security, and reduce administrative overhead. However, if roles are poorly designed, organizations may face issues such as role explosion, privilege creep, and inefficient access control processes. Implementing best practices in role engineering is essential to creating a scalable and maintainable RBAC framework.

The first step in role engineering is understanding business processes and job functions. Organizations must analyze how employees, applications, and systems interact with different resources. This requires close collaboration between IT, security teams, and business units to identify the access needs of each department. A comprehensive analysis helps define roles that accurately reflect job responsibilities while ensuring that employees receive only the necessary permissions to perform their duties. Without this initial assessment, roles may be created arbitrarily, leading to redundant or overly permissive access rights.

A key best practice in role engineering is maintaining the principle of least privilege (PoLP). Roles should be designed to provide users with the minimum level of access required to complete their tasks. Overly broad roles that grant excessive permissions can lead to security vulnerabilities, increasing the risk of unauthorized access or data breaches. To enforce PoLP, organizations should carefully map job functions to specific permissions and ensure that roles do not grant unnecessary access to sensitive systems or data.

Role hierarchies and inheritance should be leveraged to reduce redundancy and simplify role management. Instead of defining each role separately, organizations can create a structured role hierarchy where higher-level roles inherit permissions from lower-level roles. For example, a "Manager" role can inherit the permissions of an "Employee" role while adding additional privileges required for managerial tasks. Role inheritance eliminates the need to manually assign duplicate permissions, reducing complexity and ensuring consistency across the organization.

One of the biggest challenges in role engineering is avoiding role explosion. Role explosion occurs when too many roles are created to accommodate specific exceptions or unique access requirements. This issue makes role management difficult and increases administrative overhead. To prevent role explosion, organizations should focus on defining general roles that cover common job functions rather than creating highly specialized roles for individual users. If exceptions arise, they should be handled through temporary access grants or attribute-based controls rather than creating new roles for every unique case.

Regular role reviews and audits are essential to maintaining an effective RBAC system. Over time, business needs change, and employees may transition between roles or leave the organization. Without regular reviews, roles can become outdated, leading to privilege creep—where users accumulate unnecessary access rights. Conducting periodic access reviews ensures that roles remain relevant, permissions are appropriately assigned, and users do not retain access beyond their job requirements. Automated identity governance solutions can help streamline this process by identifying and flagging excessive or outdated access.

Role mining is a valuable technique for defining and refining roles based on actual usage patterns. Role mining involves analyzing access logs, user activity, and permission assignments to identify common access patterns across different job functions. By leveraging data-driven insights, organizations can create role structures that align with real-world access needs rather than making assumptions about which permissions users require. Role mining tools can also detect anomalies, such as users with excessive or unnecessary permissions, helping to refine role definitions over time.

Organizations should implement a clear role lifecycle management process to ensure that roles are created, modified, and retired as needed. A well-defined role lifecycle includes approval workflows for new role creation, criteria for modifying existing roles, and procedures for decommissioning roles that are no longer relevant. This structured approach prevents role sprawl and ensures that access control policies remain aligned with business operations. Role lifecycle management should be integrated with onboarding and offboarding processes to ensure that users are assigned the correct roles when they join an organization and that access is revoked when they leave.

Automation plays a critical role in effective role engineering. Manual role assignment and management can be time-consuming and prone to human error. By integrating RBAC with identity and access management (IAM) solutions, organizations can automate role provisioning, de-provisioning, and enforcement of access policies. Automated role-based access management improves efficiency, reduces administrative burden, and ensures consistency in access control enforcement.

To improve flexibility and adapt to dynamic access requirements, organizations may consider hybrid access control models that combine RBAC with Attribute-Based Access Control (ABAC). While RBAC provides a structured framework for managing static permissions, ABAC introduces contextual attributes such as user location, device security status, and time of access to make dynamic access decisions. This hybrid approach enhances security by allowing organizations to enforce more granular access controls while still benefiting from the simplicity of role-based management.

Training and awareness are also crucial for successful role engineering. IT administrators, security teams, and business managers must understand the purpose of roles, how they are assigned, and the importance of maintaining proper access control. Without proper training, role definitions may be inconsistent, leading to security gaps or inefficient access management. Organizations should provide clear documentation on role assignments, approval processes, and best practices to ensure that all stakeholders understand their responsibilities in maintaining RBAC.

Role engineering is an ongoing process that requires continuous refinement to keep up with organizational changes, evolving security threats, and regulatory compliance requirements. Organizations should establish a governance framework that includes defined policies for role management, regular access reviews, and automated enforcement of access policies. By following best practices in role engineering, organizations can create a scalable, efficient, and secure RBAC system that minimizes security risks while supporting operational efficiency.

Role Explosion: Challenges and Solutions

Role explosion is a common challenge in Role-Based Access Control (RBAC) systems that occurs when an excessive number of roles are created to accommodate different access needs. As organizations expand and evolve, they may find themselves managing hundreds or even thousands of roles, leading to increased administrative complexity, security risks, and inefficiencies. Role explosion undermines the very purpose of RBAC by making role management cumbersome and difficult to maintain. Addressing this challenge requires a combination of strategic role design, automation, and governance to ensure that access control remains scalable and effective.

The primary cause of role explosion is the tendency to create overly granular roles to meet specific user requirements. In many organizations, IT administrators attempt to address every unique access scenario by defining a new role rather than modifying existing ones. This results in a proliferation of roles that are difficult to track, maintain, and audit. When too many roles exist, the original goal of RBAC—simplifying access management—becomes lost in an overwhelming number of role definitions.

Another contributing factor to role explosion is the failure to establish a standardized role design process. Without a structured methodology for defining roles, different departments or teams may create their own roles independently, leading to redundancy and inconsistency. In large enterprises, this lack of coordination can result in multiple roles that serve nearly identical functions but differ slightly due to variations in naming conventions or access permissions. This redundancy not only complicates administration but also increases the risk of incorrect access assignments.

Mergers and acquisitions can also lead to role explosion. When organizations integrate IT systems, they often merge RBAC models from different business units, leading to overlapping roles with similar permissions. Without careful role consolidation, the number of roles continues to grow, creating inefficiencies and security risks. In many cases, organizations inherit legacy roles that no longer serve a functional purpose but remain in the system, further complicating access management.

One of the major risks associated with role explosion is privilege creep. When too many roles exist, users may accumulate multiple roles over time, gradually gaining excessive privileges that exceed what is necessary for their job functions. Privilege creep increases the likelihood of unauthorized access and security breaches, as users may retain access to sensitive systems long after their responsibilities have changed. The more roles an organization has, the harder it becomes to monitor and enforce the principle of least privilege (PoLP).

The complexity introduced by role explosion also impacts compliance and auditing. Regulatory frameworks such as GDPR, HIPAA, and SOX require organizations to maintain strict access controls and audit trails. When an excessive number of roles exist, tracking user permissions and demonstrating compliance becomes difficult. Security teams struggle to identify which roles are necessary, which ones are redundant, and whether users have appropriate access. Auditing thousands of roles for compliance reviews is time-consuming and increases the risk of human error.

Addressing role explosion requires a systematic approach to role consolidation and optimization. One of the most effective strategies is role mining, a process that analyzes existing access patterns to identify commonalities among users. Role mining tools use data analytics to detect redundant roles, suggest optimizations, and help organizations define a streamlined set of roles that align with actual business needs. By grouping similar roles and eliminating unnecessary ones, organizations can significantly reduce role complexity while maintaining security.

Implementing a role hierarchy is another solution to mitigate role explosion. Instead of creating separate roles for every variation of access, organizations can define parent-child relationships between roles, allowing higher-level roles to inherit permissions from lower-level ones. For example, a "Senior Engineer" role can inherit permissions from a "Junior Engineer" role, reducing the need to create multiple standalone roles for different seniority levels. Role hierarchies simplify management and ensure that access control remains structured and scalable.

Attribute-Based Access Control (ABAC) can also be integrated with RBAC to reduce role explosion. While RBAC assigns permissions based on predefined roles, ABAC introduces attributes such as department, job title, location, and device security posture to dynamically control access. By incorporating ABAC elements, organizations can avoid creating separate roles for every possible scenario. For example, instead of defining individual roles for "Remote Employee" and "On-Site Employee," an organization can use attributes to determine access dynamically based on the user's location.

Automating role lifecycle management is essential for preventing role explosion. Organizations should establish governance frameworks that define clear criteria for creating, modifying, and retiring roles. Automated identity and access management (IAM) solutions can enforce role policies, ensure that new roles meet predefined standards, and periodically review role relevance. Automation reduces administrative burden, prevents the accumulation of unnecessary roles, and helps maintain a clean and efficient RBAC system.

Regular access reviews and role audits are crucial for keeping role explosion in check. Organizations should conduct periodic role reviews to identify obsolete roles, merge redundant ones, and remove unnecessary permissions. These reviews should involve collaboration between IT security teams, department managers, and compliance officers to ensure that role definitions align with current business needs. Access certification campaigns, where users and managers review assigned roles, can help validate that roles remain appropriate over time.

Standardizing role definitions and naming conventions also contributes to role optimization. When roles are created inconsistently, administrators may struggle to distinguish between similar roles, leading to unnecessary duplication. Organizations should establish clear guidelines for naming roles, structuring permissions, and defining role scopes to maintain clarity and avoid redundant role creation. A well-documented role catalog can serve as a reference point, preventing departments from creating roles that already exist under different names.

Another effective measure to control role explosion is the adoption of just-in-time (JIT) access. Instead of permanently assigning roles with elevated privileges, JIT access grants temporary permissions only when needed. Users can request access to specific roles for a limited duration, reducing the need for static role assignments that contribute to role bloat. JIT access enhances security by ensuring that elevated permissions are only active for the necessary period, minimizing the risk of privilege abuse.

Organizations that successfully manage role explosion benefit from a more efficient, scalable, and secure access control system. By implementing best practices such as role mining, hierarchical role structures, ABAC integration, automation, and regular audits, organizations can maintain an RBAC framework that is both manageable and aligned with business objectives. Controlling role growth ensures that access control remains effective, reducing security risks and administrative overhead while improving compliance and operational efficiency.

RBAC Implementation in Enterprise Systems

Implementing Role-Based Access Control (RBAC) in enterprise systems is a complex but essential process for managing user access efficiently and securely. Large organizations handle vast amounts of sensitive data, applications, and infrastructure components, making it critical to enforce structured access control policies. RBAC provides a scalable approach by granting permissions based on roles instead of assigning them directly to users. This reduces administrative overhead, improves security, and ensures compliance with regulatory requirements.

A successful RBAC implementation begins with a thorough analysis of business processes and user responsibilities. Organizations must identify the different job functions that exist within the company and determine the access requirements for each role. This involves working closely with department heads, IT administrators, and security teams to map out workflows, data access needs, and system dependencies. Without a clear understanding of business operations, RBAC implementation can result in excessive permissions, inefficiencies, and security vulnerabilities.

Once job functions are defined, organizations must establish a standardized role hierarchy. A well-structured RBAC model organizes roles in a way that higher-level roles inherit permissions from lower-level roles, reducing redundancy and simplifying management. For example, an "IT Support Engineer" role may include basic access to user management tools, while a "Senior IT Administrator" role may inherit those permissions and add access to critical system configurations. Proper role structuring ensures that employees receive only the necessary level of access without unnecessary privilege escalation.

One of the biggest challenges in RBAC implementation is avoiding role explosion, where too many roles are created to accommodate slight variations in user permissions. To mitigate this issue, organizations should focus on defining broad roles that encompass common access requirements rather than creating overly granular roles. If exceptions arise, temporary access mechanisms, such as just-in-time (JIT) access or Attribute-Based Access Control (ABAC) overlays, can be used instead of creating additional roles. Regular role reviews and audits also help prevent excessive role proliferation.

Role mining is a useful technique in RBAC implementation, allowing organizations to analyze existing access patterns and identify common permission groupings. By examining historical access logs and user behavior, security teams can define roles based on real-world data rather than assumptions. Role mining tools use data analytics to detect redundant permissions, propose optimal role structures, and highlight inconsistencies in access assignments. This approach streamlines role creation and ensures that roles accurately reflect operational needs.

Integration with Identity and Access Management (IAM) solutions is a crucial aspect of RBAC deployment in enterprise environments. IAM platforms centralize user authentication, authorization, and provisioning, enabling organizations to enforce RBAC policies consistently across all systems. By integrating RBAC with IAM, organizations can automate user role assignments, synchronize role changes with HR systems, and streamline access reviews. Automated provisioning ensures that employees receive appropriate access when they join the company, and de-provisioning removes access when they leave, reducing the risk of orphaned accounts.

RBAC implementation must also account for Separation of Duties (SoD) policies to prevent conflicts of interest and security risks. SoD ensures that critical tasks are divided among multiple users, preventing any single individual from having unchecked control over sensitive operations. For example, in financial systems, the person responsible for processing payments should not have the authority to approve them. RBAC enforces SoD by structuring roles in a way that restricts conflicting permissions, reducing the risk of fraud and internal threats.

Enforcing RBAC policies across cloud and hybrid environments presents additional challenges. Enterprises often operate in multi-cloud ecosystems with users accessing applications from different locations and devices. Cloud-based IAM solutions, such as Microsoft Azure Active Directory, AWS IAM, and Google Cloud IAM, provide built-in RBAC capabilities that allow organizations to define role-based access policies for cloud resources. However, ensuring consistent RBAC enforcement across on-premises and cloud environments requires unified policy management and cross-platform integration.

RBAC implementation also plays a key role in regulatory compliance. Many industry regulations, such as the General Data Protection Regulation (GDPR), the Health Insurance Portability and Accountability Act (HIPAA), and the Sarbanes-Oxley Act (SOX), mandate strict access controls to protect sensitive information. RBAC helps enterprises meet compliance requirements by enforcing least privilege access, maintaining audit trails, and providing a clear framework for access governance. Regular access certification reviews and automated reporting tools further enhance compliance efforts.

User training and awareness are critical for a successful RBAC deployment. Employees must understand the importance of access control policies, how role assignments affect their permissions, and the process for requesting additional access if needed. Clear documentation, self-service access request portals, and helpdesk support improve user adoption and reduce confusion. Without proper training, users may inadvertently bypass RBAC controls by sharing credentials or requesting unnecessary privileges, undermining security efforts.

Monitoring and auditing are essential components of RBAC implementation. Organizations must continuously track access requests, role modifications, and permission usage to detect anomalies or unauthorized privilege escalations. Security Information and Event Management (SIEM) solutions provide real-time visibility into access patterns, helping organizations identify suspicious activity and enforce security policies proactively. Automated alerting mechanisms can flag unauthorized access attempts, policy violations, or inactive roles that should be decommissioned.

Continuous improvement is necessary to maintain an effective RBAC system. Business operations evolve over time, requiring periodic role adjustments to reflect organizational changes. Regular access reviews, role optimizations, and policy refinements ensure that RBAC remains aligned with business needs. Organizations should establish governance frameworks that define role lifecycle management, access approval workflows, and audit procedures to keep RBAC policies up to date.

RBAC implementation in enterprise systems is a strategic initiative that enhances security, improves operational efficiency, and ensures regulatory compliance. By defining well-structured roles, leveraging automation, integrating with IAM platforms, and enforcing access governance, organizations can successfully deploy RBAC at scale. With continuous monitoring and refinement, RBAC remains an effective solution for managing access in complex IT environments while reducing administrative burdens and security risks.

RBAC in Cloud and Hybrid Environments

Role-Based Access Control (RBAC) is a fundamental security model for managing user permissions across enterprise systems. As organizations increasingly adopt cloud and hybrid environments, implementing RBAC becomes more complex due to the distributed nature of resources, dynamic workloads, and multi-cloud architectures. While traditional RBAC models were designed for on-premises systems with well-defined boundaries, cloud environments require a more flexible and scalable approach to access control. Ensuring consistency in RBAC policies across hybrid infrastructures is essential for maintaining security, operational efficiency, and regulatory compliance.

In a cloud environment, RBAC provides a structured way to control access to cloud resources based on predefined roles. Cloud providers such as Amazon Web Services (AWS), Microsoft Azure, and Google Cloud Platform (GCP) offer built-in RBAC mechanisms that allow organizations to define roles and assign permissions based on least privilege principles. Unlike traditional on-premises RBAC, cloud-based RBAC extends across multiple services, including virtual machines, databases, storage, networking, and APIs. This makes it crucial for administrators to carefully define roles to prevent excessive permissions that could lead to security vulnerabilities.

Hybrid environments introduce additional complexity by requiring RBAC policies to be enforced across both on-premises infrastructure and cloud services. Many enterprises operate in hybrid models where legacy systems coexist with modern cloud platforms. This necessitates integration between existing RBAC frameworks and cloud-based IAM solutions to maintain consistency in access control policies. Without proper alignment, discrepancies between on-premises and cloud access controls can create security gaps, leading to unauthorized access or compliance violations.

One of the key challenges in implementing RBAC in cloud and hybrid environments is managing role consistency across different platforms. Each cloud provider has its own RBAC implementation, with varying levels of granularity and role definitions. For example, AWS uses Identity and Access Management (IAM) roles, Azure implements role-based access control (Azure RBAC), and GCP offers IAM policies. While these services provide similar functionality, their role structures and permission models differ, making it challenging for organizations to create a unified RBAC framework across multiple cloud providers.

To address this challenge, organizations can implement centralized identity and access management (IAM) solutions that integrate with multiple cloud platforms. Federated identity management allows users to authenticate once and access resources across different environments using a single identity. By leveraging IAM solutions such as Okta, Microsoft Entra ID (formerly Azure Active Directory), or Ping Identity, organizations can enforce consistent RBAC policies across hybrid infrastructures. These solutions provide role mapping, policy enforcement, and identity federation, reducing the complexity of managing disparate RBAC implementations.

Another important consideration in cloud-based RBAC is the dynamic nature of cloud workloads. Unlike static on-premises environments, cloud resources are often provisioned and deprovisioned on demand. This means that RBAC policies must be flexible enough to accommodate changing resource requirements without introducing security risks. Organizations should implement automated role provisioning and deprovisioning mechanisms to ensure that temporary workloads receive appropriate permissions without persistent over-privileged access.

RBAC in cloud environments also extends to service accounts and non-human identities. Many cloud services and applications require permissions to access resources, making it essential to apply RBAC principles to machine identities, API keys, and service accounts. Without proper governance, misconfigured service accounts can become security liabilities, granting excessive privileges that attackers can exploit. Organizations should regularly audit service account permissions, restrict access based on least privilege, and implement just-in-time (JIT) access to limit exposure.

Multi-cloud environments further complicate RBAC implementation by requiring organizations to manage roles across different cloud platforms with varying access control models. A common approach to solving this issue is using cloud access security brokers (CASBs) or cloud governance platforms to enforce unified RBAC policies across multiple clouds. These tools provide visibility into access permissions, enforce policy consistency, and help detect misconfigurations that could lead to security incidents.

Compliance and auditing play a crucial role in RBAC implementation in cloud and hybrid environments. Regulations such as GDPR, HIPAA, and SOC 2 require organizations to enforce strict access controls and maintain audit logs of user activity. Cloud providers offer logging and monitoring capabilities that allow organizations to track RBAC-related events, including role assignments, access attempts, and policy changes. Security Information and Event Management (SIEM) solutions can aggregate these logs, providing real-time insights into access control violations and suspicious activities.

RBAC in hybrid environments requires careful coordination between on-premises Active Directory (AD) and cloud-based IAM services. Many enterprises extend their existing AD infrastructure to the cloud, allowing on-premises identities to authenticate with cloud services using single sign-on (SSO) and federated authentication. Hybrid RBAC implementations must ensure that role mappings between AD groups and cloud roles are correctly defined to prevent access inconsistencies. Misaligned role assignments can lead to excessive privileges in one environment while restricting necessary access in another.

Automation and policy enforcement are critical to maintaining RBAC integrity in cloud environments. Organizations should implement infrastructure-as-code (IaC) practices to define RBAC policies programmatically. Using tools like Terraform, AWS CloudFormation, or Azure Bicep, security teams can codify role definitions, permission assignments, and access policies as version-controlled code. This approach ensures that RBAC configurations are applied consistently across environments and can be audited or rolled back if necessary.

Another best practice for cloud-based RBAC is the use of conditional access policies. Many cloud providers allow organizations to enforce access controls based on contextual factors such as device compliance, network location, or risk level. Conditional access enhances RBAC by introducing dynamic authorization decisions that adapt to changing security conditions. For example, an RBAC policy might grant access to a role only if the user is connecting from a trusted device within an approved geographic region.

To maintain an effective RBAC implementation in cloud and hybrid environments, organizations should conduct regular access reviews and role audits. Cloud environments evolve rapidly, and permissions granted months ago may no longer be necessary. Implementing periodic access certification campaigns ensures that roles remain aligned with business requirements and that excessive permissions are revoked. IAM automation tools can assist in detecting unused roles, flagging policy violations, and recommending role optimizations.

Organizations adopting RBAC in cloud and hybrid environments must also prepare for the shift towards Zero Trust security models. Traditional perimeter-based security approaches are no longer sufficient in cloud-centric architectures. Zero Trust principles require continuous verification of user identities, strict least-privilege enforcement, and ongoing monitoring of access patterns. RBAC remains a foundational component of Zero Trust, but it must be supplemented with real-time risk assessments, behavioral analytics, and adaptive access controls.

Effective RBAC implementation in cloud and hybrid environments requires a balance between security, flexibility, and operational efficiency. Organizations must adopt a strategic approach that includes identity federation, automation, centralized policy management, and continuous monitoring. By aligning RBAC policies with modern cloud security frameworks, enterprises can protect sensitive resources, reduce administrative overhead, and maintain compliance across distributed IT landscapes.

Managing Role Assignments and Lifecycle

Effective management of role assignments and lifecycle is essential for maintaining a secure and efficient Role-Based Access Control (RBAC) system. Organizations rely on RBAC to control access to sensitive data and systems, ensuring that users receive appropriate permissions based on their job functions. However, without proper governance, role assignments can become inconsistent, leading to security risks such as privilege creep, excessive access, and orphaned accounts. Managing role assignments and their lifecycle requires a structured approach that includes automated provisioning, continuous monitoring, regular audits, and deprovisioning processes.

The role assignment process begins when a user joins an organization or changes job responsibilities. Assigning the correct roles to employees is crucial to ensuring they can perform their tasks without unnecessary access privileges. Role assignments should be based on predefined access control policies that align with business functions and security requirements. Instead of granting permissions directly to users, organizations should leverage role mappings that associate job titles, departments, and responsibilities with specific roles. This approach minimizes the risk of human error and enforces consistency in access management.

Automation plays a critical role in managing role assignments efficiently. Manual role provisioning is time-consuming, prone to errors, and difficult to scale in large enterprises. Identity and Access Management (IAM) systems streamline the process by automating role assignments based on HR records, organizational policies, and predefined workflows. When a new employee is onboarded, their role can be automatically assigned based on their job title and department, ensuring they receive the necessary access immediately. This automation reduces administrative overhead and enhances security by preventing delays or misconfigurations in access provisioning.

One of the biggest challenges in role assignment is preventing privilege creep, which occurs when users accumulate excessive permissions over time. Employees who change roles or take on temporary assignments may receive additional roles without having their previous access rights revoked. If not managed properly, this can lead to security vulnerabilities, where users retain access to systems they no longer need. Organizations should implement regular access reviews to identify and remove unnecessary roles, ensuring that users only have the permissions required for their current responsibilities.

Role lifecycle management extends beyond initial role assignment and includes role modifications, temporary access, and deprovisioning. As business needs evolve, roles must be updated to reflect changes in job functions, regulatory requirements, or security policies. Organizations should establish a governance framework that defines how roles are created, modified, and retired. This ensures that roles remain relevant, effective, and aligned with organizational objectives. Role modifications should follow a formal approval process, with security teams and business stakeholders involved in reviewing changes before implementation.

Temporary access management is another critical aspect of role lifecycle management. In some cases, employees or contractors may require short-term access to specific resources for projects, audits, or troubleshooting. Instead of assigning permanent roles that could lead to excessive permissions, organizations should use Just-In-Time (JIT) access controls or time-bound role assignments. These mechanisms ensure that access is granted only for a specified period and automatically revoked once it is no longer needed. JIT access reduces the risk of long-term privilege accumulation and enhances security by limiting exposure to sensitive systems.

Deprovisioning is a key component of role lifecycle management, ensuring that access is revoked when employees leave the organization or change job roles. Failing to deprovision access in a timely manner can lead to security risks such as insider threats and orphaned accounts—accounts that remain active even though the associated user no longer requires access. Automated deprovisioning workflows help organizations quickly remove roles and permissions when an employee departs, preventing unauthorized access to corporate resources.

Regular role audits and access certification campaigns help maintain an effective RBAC system by validating that assigned roles are still appropriate. Organizations should conduct periodic reviews to identify outdated roles, inactive accounts, and excessive permissions. During an access certification campaign, managers and security teams review employee access rights, verifying that each user has the correct level of access. If discrepancies are found, corrective actions such as revoking unnecessary roles or modifying permissions should be taken immediately.

To further optimize role lifecycle management, organizations should consider role consolidation to reduce complexity and prevent role explosion. Over time, organizations may accumulate too many roles with overlapping permissions, making it difficult to manage access efficiently. Role mining techniques, which analyze historical access patterns and permission assignments, can help identify redundant roles and streamline the role structure. By consolidating similar roles, organizations can simplify role management while maintaining security and compliance.

Integration with governance, risk, and compliance (GRC) frameworks enhances role lifecycle management by ensuring that access control policies align with regulatory requirements. Many industries, such as finance, healthcare, and government, must adhere to strict access control regulations, including GDPR, HIPAA, and SOX. By implementing role-based governance policies, organizations can enforce compliance, reduce audit complexities, and mitigate security risks.

User behavior analytics (UBA) and artificial intelligence (AI) are emerging technologies that can improve role assignment and lifecycle management. AI-driven analytics can detect anomalies in role usage, flagging cases where users have excessive privileges or unused roles. For example, if a user has access to a financial reporting system but has not used it for several months, the system can trigger a review or recommend revocation of access. These intelligent access management capabilities help organizations proactively manage role assignments and enhance security posture.

Training and awareness programs also contribute to effective role management by educating employees on access control best practices. Employees should understand the importance of role-based access, the risks of privilege misuse, and the procedures for requesting additional access. Security teams should communicate clear guidelines on role assignments, access request workflows, and role escalation policies. Ensuring that users and administrators are well-informed reduces the likelihood of misconfigured roles and improves overall security.

Managing role assignments and lifecycle requires a balance between security, operational efficiency, and compliance. By implementing automation, enforcing regular access reviews, and integrating advanced analytics, organizations can maintain a structured and secure RBAC system. A well-managed role lifecycle not only minimizes security risks but also enhances business agility by ensuring that users receive appropriate access at the right time while preventing excessive or outdated permissions.

Compliance and Audit Considerations in RBAC

Role-Based Access Control (RBAC) plays a critical role in ensuring that organizations meet regulatory compliance requirements and maintain a secure access control framework. Many industries are subject to strict regulations that mandate proper management of user access to sensitive data and systems. Compliance frameworks such as the General Data Protection Regulation (GDPR), the Health Insurance Portability and Accountability Act (HIPAA), the Sarbanes-Oxley Act (SOX), and the Payment Card Industry Data Security Standard (PCI DSS) require organizations to implement robust access controls, restrict unauthorized access, and conduct regular audits. Proper RBAC implementation helps organizations demonstrate compliance while reducing security risks associated with excessive or mismanaged permissions.

One of the primary compliance considerations in RBAC is enforcing the principle of least privilege (PoLP). This principle ensures that users have only the minimum permissions necessary to perform their tasks. Many regulatory frameworks require organizations to apply strict access controls to protect personal, financial, and healthcare data. RBAC simplifies the enforcement of least privilege by defining roles based on job responsibilities, ensuring that users do not receive excessive access that could lead to data breaches or regulatory violations.

Another important compliance requirement is access segregation and separation of duties (SoD). Many regulations mandate that critical business functions must be divided among multiple individuals to prevent fraud, unauthorized changes, and conflicts of interest. For example, in financial systems, the person responsible for creating transactions should not have the authority to approve them. RBAC enables organizations to enforce SoD by structuring role assignments in a way that prevents conflicts and ensures that no single individual has unrestricted control over sensitive processes.

Access certification and periodic reviews are essential audit requirements for demonstrating compliance. Regulatory bodies require organizations to periodically review access permissions to ensure that only authorized users retain access to sensitive data and systems. RBAC facilitates access reviews by providing a structured framework that maps roles to permissions, making it easier to verify whether user access aligns with business and security policies. Organizations should conduct periodic role-based access reviews, removing unnecessary privileges and revoking access for users who no longer require it.

Auditing plays a key role in ensuring that RBAC policies are being followed correctly. Organizations must maintain detailed access logs and audit trails to track user activity, monitor access requests, and identify any unauthorized actions. Audit logs should record critical events such as role assignments, permission changes, access approvals, and failed login attempts. Security Information and Event Management (SIEM) systems can aggregate and analyze access logs in real time, helping organizations detect suspicious activity and respond to security incidents promptly.

To ensure compliance, organizations must establish RBAC governance policies that define how access control is managed, reviewed, and enforced. Governance frameworks should outline the process for role creation, modification, and deactivation, ensuring that roles remain relevant and aligned with compliance requirements. Clear documentation of role definitions, role hierarchies, and approval workflows helps organizations maintain transparency and accountability in access management.

One of the challenges organizations face in maintaining RBAC compliance is role explosion, where an excessive number of roles are created to accommodate different access needs. This can make access reviews difficult and increase the risk of misconfigurations. To address this, organizations should regularly consolidate and refine roles, ensuring that they remain manageable and aligned with compliance requirements. Role mining techniques can help identify redundant roles and streamline access control policies.

Automated role provisioning and deprovisioning is another crucial compliance requirement. Many regulations mandate that access must be promptly revoked when employees leave an organization or change job roles. Delayed access revocation can lead to security risks, such as insider threats or unauthorized data access. IAM solutions integrated with RBAC enable automated role provisioning based on HR data, ensuring that access is granted or revoked in real time as employees join, move, or leave the organization.

Multi-factor authentication (MFA) and access control policies enhance RBAC compliance by adding additional layers of security. Some regulations require organizations to implement MFA for accessing sensitive systems, reducing the risk of unauthorized access due to stolen credentials. Organizations can integrate RBAC with MFA policies, ensuring that users must verify their identities before accessing critical systems or performing high-risk actions. Conditional access policies can further strengthen security by restricting access based on factors such as device compliance, geographic location, or time of access.

For organizations operating in cloud and hybrid environments, RBAC compliance must extend across multiple platforms. Cloud service providers offer RBAC capabilities that help enforce access controls, but organizations must ensure that RBAC policies are consistently applied across on-premises, cloud, and multi-cloud environments. Cloud governance tools, identity federation, and centralized IAM platforms can help maintain RBAC consistency, reducing compliance risks associated with fragmented access control models.

Regular compliance audits and assessments help organizations validate their RBAC implementation against regulatory requirements. Internal audits should assess whether roles are properly assigned, access reviews are conducted on schedule, and logs are maintained accurately. External audits, conducted by third-party compliance assessors, provide independent verification that RBAC policies meet industry standards. Organizations should prepare for audits by maintaining up-to-date access control documentation, generating audit reports, and demonstrating compliance with security controls.

Organizations should also implement incident response and access control remediation plans to address compliance violations. If an audit identifies unauthorized access, excessive permissions, or security gaps, organizations must have a process in place to remediate issues quickly.

This may involve revoking inappropriate access, adjusting role definitions, implementing additional monitoring, or enhancing training for access management teams. A well-defined remediation process ensures that organizations can respond to compliance risks proactively.

Effective RBAC implementation supports data protection and privacy compliance by ensuring that access to sensitive data is restricted to authorized individuals. Regulations such as GDPR impose strict requirements on how organizations handle personal data, including limiting access to only those who need it for legitimate purposes. By enforcing RBAC policies that restrict data access based on roles, organizations reduce the risk of unauthorized exposure and ensure compliance with privacy laws.

Training and awareness are essential for ensuring that employees understand RBAC compliance requirements. IT administrators, security teams, and business managers must be trained on access control policies, audit requirements, and compliance best practices. Employees should also be educated on security awareness topics such as phishing, password hygiene, and responsible access management. An informed workforce reduces the likelihood of accidental compliance violations and strengthens overall security.

Maintaining RBAC compliance requires a continuous effort that involves governance, automation, auditing, and policy enforcement. By implementing strong access control policies, regularly reviewing role assignments, integrating automated identity management solutions, and conducting compliance audits, organizations can effectively manage RBAC while meeting regulatory requirements. A well-governed RBAC system not only enhances security but also ensures transparency, accountability, and alignment with industry standards.

RBAC Case Studies: Successes and Failures

Role-Based Access Control (RBAC) has been widely implemented across industries to manage access control efficiently and enhance security. Many organizations have successfully deployed RBAC to enforce the principle of least privilege, streamline compliance, and reduce administrative overhead. However, some implementations have faced significant challenges, leading to security risks, operational inefficiencies, and compliance failures. Examining real-world case studies of RBAC implementations provides valuable insights into best practices and common pitfalls.

One of the most notable success stories of RBAC implementation comes from a global financial institution that needed to improve security and compliance with financial regulations such as the Sarbanes-Oxley Act (SOX). Before RBAC, the organization struggled with excessive permissions, where employees retained access to systems long after switching roles or departments. This led to privilege creep, increasing the risk of insider threats.

To address these issues, the company implemented an RBAC framework that mapped job functions to specific roles, ensuring that employees received only the necessary permissions. Role hierarchies were established to streamline access across departments, and a governance structure was put in place to conduct periodic access reviews. By automating role provisioning and integrating RBAC with its identity and access management (IAM) system, the company reduced access misconfigurations and improved compliance. As a result, the organization successfully passed regulatory audits with minimal findings, reduced security risks, and improved operational efficiency by simplifying role assignments.

In contrast, an RBAC failure case involved a healthcare provider that attempted to implement RBAC to meet HIPAA compliance requirements. The organization sought to restrict access to patient records based on job roles to prevent unauthorized disclosures. However, the RBAC deployment encountered several issues due to poor planning and lack of stakeholder involvement.

One of the primary challenges was role explosion, where the organization created hundreds of roles to accommodate minor variations in job functions. This excessive role granularity made it difficult for administrators to manage access effectively. Additionally, the organization failed to conduct proper role mining before implementation, leading to redundant and overlapping roles. Over time, employees accumulated multiple roles, resulting in excessive permissions that contradicted the intended security goals.

Moreover, the organization lacked an automated role management system, making it difficult to revoke access when employees changed roles or left the organization. This led to orphaned accounts with active permissions, violating HIPAA regulations. The failure of the RBAC implementation ultimately resulted in a data breach when an unauthorized employee accessed and leaked sensitive patient records. After an investigation, the healthcare provider was fined for non-compliance and had to overhaul its access control policies, reducing role complexity and implementing automated role deprovisioning.

Another successful RBAC implementation was seen in a large manufacturing company that needed to secure access to its operational technology (OT) systems. The company had thousands of employees across multiple locations, making it challenging to enforce consistent access policies. Before implementing RBAC, system administrators had to manually assign permissions for each user, leading to delays and security risks.

To improve access control, the organization designed a structured RBAC model that grouped users based on job responsibilities, department, and geographic location. A central IAM system was integrated with the RBAC framework to automate role assignments, reducing the burden on IT administrators. The organization also adopted Just-In-Time (JIT) access, ensuring that elevated privileges were granted only when necessary and revoked automatically after use.

This implementation improved operational efficiency by reducing manual workload, strengthened security by minimizing unnecessary access, and helped the company comply with industry regulations. Additionally, the RBAC model supported the company's digital transformation strategy, allowing seamless integration with cloud services and remote access solutions.

However, not all RBAC implementations succeed due to technical limitations or organizational resistance. A notable failure case involved a government agency that attempted to deploy RBAC to control access to classified information. The project was highly ambitious, aiming to consolidate access control across multiple departments with different security requirements.

The main issue was lack of executive buy-in and user adoption. The RBAC model was designed without consulting department heads and end-users, leading to resistance from employees who found the new access restrictions cumbersome. Many users struggled with role-based restrictions that prevented them from performing legitimate job functions, leading to frequent access request escalations.

Additionally, the agency underestimated the complexity of mapping roles to existing policies, resulting in delays and inconsistencies in role definitions. Without proper change management, employees attempted to bypass RBAC controls by sharing credentials, undermining the security model. Eventually, the agency had to revise its access control strategy, incorporating a hybrid model that combined RBAC with Attribute-Based Access Control (ABAC) to provide more flexibility in access decisions.

One of the key lessons from these case studies is that successful RBAC implementation requires careful planning, automation, and continuous monitoring. Organizations that conduct thorough role mining, define clear role hierarchies, and integrate RBAC with IAM solutions are more likely to achieve their security and compliance objectives. Additionally, involving stakeholders from the beginning and providing user training can improve adoption and reduce resistance to change.

Conversely, organizations that fail to manage RBAC complexity, neglect automation, or overlook stakeholder involvement often struggle with scalability and security issues. Role explosion, privilege creep, and orphaned accounts are common risks that undermine the effectiveness of RBAC if not properly addressed. Organizations must conduct regular access reviews, enforce least privilege principles, and integrate automation to maintain a well-functioning RBAC system.

By learning from both successful and failed implementations, organizations can develop a strategic approach to RBAC deployment that balances security, compliance, and operational efficiency. Whether securing financial transactions, protecting patient data, or managing access to critical infrastructure, RBAC remains a powerful access control model—provided it is implemented with the right governance, automation, and oversight.

Automating RBAC with Identity Governance

Role-Based Access Control (RBAC) provides organizations with a structured framework for managing user access, but manually administering roles and permissions can be time-consuming, error-prone, and difficult to scale. As enterprises grow and IT environments become more complex, automating RBAC through identity governance solutions becomes essential. Identity governance ensures that access control policies are consistently enforced, that user permissions remain aligned with business needs, and that compliance requirements are met. By integrating RBAC with identity governance platforms, organizations can streamline role management, improve security, and reduce administrative overhead.

Identity governance encompasses the processes, policies, and technologies that manage user identities and access within an organization. It goes beyond traditional Identity and Access Management (IAM) by providing visibility into user entitlements, enforcing compliance controls, and enabling automated access reviews. When combined with RBAC, identity governance solutions allow organizations to automate role assignments, track permission changes, and enforce least privilege access without relying on manual interventions.

One of the primary benefits of automating RBAC with identity governance is automated role provisioning and deprovisioning. In traditional RBAC implementations, administrators must manually assign roles to new employees and revoke access when employees leave the organization or change job roles. This manual process introduces delays, increases the risk of human error, and creates security vulnerabilities if access is not revoked promptly. Identity governance platforms integrate with HR systems and directory services to automate the provisioning of roles based on predefined policies. When an employee joins an organization, their assigned job function determines the roles they receive, ensuring immediate and accurate access provisioning. Similarly, when an employee departs, their access is automatically deprovisioned, reducing the risk of orphaned accounts.

Another critical advantage of identity governance in RBAC automation is role mining and optimization. Over time, organizations may accumulate redundant or overly complex roles, leading to role explosion and privilege creep. Identity governance solutions use role mining techniques to analyze user access patterns and identify common role groupings. By leveraging machine learning and data analytics, these solutions suggest role consolidations, detect excessive privileges, and help security teams refine role definitions. Role optimization ensures that employees receive the correct level of access without unnecessary permissions, enhancing security while simplifying role management.

Identity governance also plays a key role in access certification and compliance audits. Many regulatory frameworks, such as GDPR, HIPAA, and SOX, require organizations to regularly review user access to ensure that only authorized individuals retain access to sensitive systems and data. Manual access reviews can be inefficient and difficult to track, particularly in large organizations. Identity governance platforms automate access certification processes by generating periodic review campaigns, notifying managers to validate user entitlements, and revoking permissions that are no longer needed. These automated reviews improve compliance by ensuring that access rights remain aligned with business policies while providing detailed audit trails for regulatory reporting.

Another important aspect of automating RBAC with identity governance is policy-based access control and role enforcement. Identity governance platforms enable organizations to define access control policies that dynamically adjust user permissions based on contextual factors such as job function, department, and security risk. These policies ensure that role assignments adhere to business rules and compliance requirements. For example, an organization may implement a policy that prevents users from holding conflicting roles, enforcing Separation of Duties (SoD) to reduce the risk of fraud or errors.

Identity governance solutions also facilitate Just-In-Time (JIT) access management, allowing users to request temporary elevated privileges when needed. Instead of assigning permanent high-privilege roles, organizations can use identity governance to grant time-limited access based on approval workflows. For instance, an IT administrator may require elevated permissions for system maintenance, but those privileges should expire automatically after the task is completed. JIT access minimizes the risk of standing privileges while maintaining operational efficiency.

Integration with cloud and hybrid environments is another significant advantage of automating RBAC with identity governance. Many organizations operate across multiple cloud platforms and on-premises systems, requiring consistent enforcement of access policies across diverse environments. Identity governance platforms provide centralized visibility and control over role assignments across cloud services such as AWS, Microsoft Azure, and Google Cloud, ensuring that RBAC policies remain uniform and effective. Cloud-native integrations enable seamless provisioning, monitoring, and policy enforcement across hybrid infrastructures.

Identity governance also enhances incident response and risk management in RBAC environments. By continuously monitoring user activities and role changes, identity governance solutions detect anomalies such as unauthorized access attempts, privilege escalations, or unusual role assignments. If a security risk is identified, automated remediation workflows can trigger actions such as revoking access, requiring multi-factor authentication (MFA), or initiating security investigations. This proactive approach reduces the likelihood of security incidents and strengthens an organization's overall cybersecurity posture.

A well-implemented identity governance framework also improves user experience and self-service access management. Employees often require additional access beyond their initially assigned roles, leading to frequent IT support requests. Identity governance solutions provide self-service portals where users can request additional roles or permissions based on pre-approved policies. These requests follow automated approval workflows, reducing administrative burden while ensuring that access requests are properly vetted. Self-service access management accelerates productivity without compromising security.

Automating RBAC with identity governance requires ongoing monitoring, governance policies, and continuous improvement.

Organizations should establish governance committees to oversee role definitions, access policies, and compliance requirements. Regular audits should be conducted to identify areas for improvement, eliminate redundant roles, and refine access control policies. Identity governance solutions provide real-time dashboards and reporting tools that help organizations assess RBAC effectiveness, track compliance metrics, and identify security gaps.

By leveraging identity governance to automate RBAC, organizations can achieve greater efficiency, enhanced security, and regulatory compliance. Automated provisioning, access reviews, policy enforcement, and risk-based monitoring ensure that RBAC remains a scalable and effective access control model. With the increasing complexity of enterprise IT environments, identity governance is essential for maintaining control over user access, preventing security risks, and supporting a zero-trust security framework. Organizations that integrate RBAC with identity governance not only streamline access management but also reduce the risk of unauthorized access, insider threats, and compliance violations.

Core Components of ABAC

Attribute-Based Access Control (ABAC) is a powerful and flexible access control model that determines access rights based on attributes rather than predefined roles. Unlike Role-Based Access Control (RBAC), which assigns permissions to users based on roles, ABAC evaluates multiple factors—such as user identity, resource characteristics, environmental conditions, and contextual attributes—to make dynamic access decisions. This approach provides organizations with fine-grained access control, enabling them to enforce security policies that adapt to real-time scenarios. Implementing ABAC requires a clear understanding of its core components, which include subjects, objects, actions, attributes, and policies.

The first fundamental component of ABAC is the subject, which represents the entity attempting to access a resource. A subject can be a human user, an application, a device, or an automated process. Unlike traditional access control models that rely only on usernames or roles, ABAC evaluates attributes associated with the subject to determine access permissions. These attributes may include job title, department, security clearance level, device type, authentication method, or any other characteristic relevant to access control decisions. By analyzing these attributes, ABAC ensures that access is granted only when specific conditions are met.

The object is another key component in ABAC and refers to the resource that a subject wants to access. Objects can include files, databases, applications, network systems, APIs, or any digital asset that requires controlled access. Each object in an ABAC system has its own set of attributes that help determine who can access it and under what conditions. For example, a confidential document may have attributes such as classification level, ownership, or encryption status, which influence access decisions. By incorporating object attributes into access control policies, ABAC allows for highly specific and contextual security measures.

The action represents the type of operation a subject wants to perform on an object. Common actions in access control systems include read, write, delete, execute, modify, or share. In ABAC, access decisions are based on whether the subject's attributes align with the object's attributes in the context of a requested action. For example, a user with an "employee" attribute might be allowed to "read" a document but not "delete" it, while a user with a "manager" attribute might have additional permissions. The ability to define access policies based on specific actions enhances security by preventing unauthorized modifications to critical data.

One of the defining characteristics of ABAC is its use of attributes to determine access control decisions. Attributes can be classified into four main categories:

Subject attributes – These describe the user or entity making the access request. Examples include name, role, department, security clearance, employment status, and authentication level.

Object attributes – These describe the resource being accessed, such as file classification, data owner, encryption status, sensitivity level, and creation date.

Action attributes – These define the operation being performed on the object, such as reading, writing, modifying, executing, or sharing.

Environmental attributes – These refer to contextual factors that influence access decisions. Examples include time of access, geographic location, network security level, device security posture, and system risk score.

By combining these attributes, ABAC enables organizations to create highly granular access control policies that consider real-world conditions. This flexibility makes ABAC particularly useful in dynamic environments such as cloud computing, healthcare, financial services, and government agencies, where access control requirements frequently change.

The policy is another critical component of ABAC and defines the rules that govern access decisions. Policies are written in a structured format that evaluates attributes and determines whether access should be granted or denied. A common policy structure follows an "if-then" logic, specifying conditions under which access is permitted. For example, a policy might state:

"If a user has a security clearance of 'Top Secret' AND is accessing the document from a corporate network AND the document is classified as 'Confidential,' THEN grant read access."

Policies in ABAC can be expressed using policy languages such as eXtensible Access Control Markup Language (XACML), which provides a standardized framework for defining and enforcing access control rules. Organizations can create complex policies that take multiple attributes into account, allowing for highly customizable security controls.

A core advantage of ABAC is its ability to support dynamic and context-aware access control. Unlike RBAC, where permissions are fixed based on role assignments, ABAC evaluates attributes in real-time, allowing access decisions to adapt to changing conditions. For instance, a healthcare provider might be allowed to access a patient's records only during their scheduled shift, or an employee may be restricted from accessing corporate resources from an untrusted network. This adaptability makes ABAC well-suited for zero-trust security models, where continuous verification is required before granting access.

Another important component of ABAC is policy enforcement and decision-making. The access control system consists of two primary entities:

Policy Enforcement Point (PEP) – The component that intercepts access requests and enforces access control decisions based on predefined policies. PEP acts as the gatekeeper, ensuring that all access attempts are evaluated against ABAC rules before granting or denying access.

Policy Decision Point (PDP) – The component that evaluates access requests against policies and attributes to make authorization decisions. PDP retrieves relevant attribute data, applies policy logic, and returns an allow or deny decision to the PEP.

The interaction between PEP and PDP ensures that access control decisions are centralized, scalable, and enforceable across distributed environments. Organizations can integrate these components with existing identity and access management (IAM) solutions to streamline authentication, authorization, and policy enforcement.

Logging and auditing are also essential components of ABAC, providing visibility into access requests and policy enforcement. Organizations must maintain detailed logs of access events, including who accessed what resources, when, and under what conditions. These logs help security teams detect anomalies, investigate security incidents, and demonstrate compliance with regulatory requirements.

Implementing ABAC requires careful planning and governance to define meaningful attributes, enforce policies consistently, and ensure that attribute data remains accurate. Organizations should establish attribute management processes, automate policy updates, and regularly review access control decisions to align with evolving security and business requirements. By leveraging the core components of ABAC, organizations can achieve a more dynamic, secure, and context-aware access control system that meets the demands of modern IT environments.

Policy Models and Expressions in ABAC

Attribute-Based Access Control (ABAC) provides a flexible and dynamic approach to managing access control policies by evaluating attributes instead of predefined roles. The foundation of ABAC lies in its policy models and expressions, which define the rules that determine whether a user can access a resource. Unlike static access control models, ABAC policies allow organizations to make real-time access decisions based on user attributes, object characteristics, environmental conditions, and contextual factors. By implementing well-structured policy models and using expressive policy languages, organizations can create granular access control rules that adapt to various security and business needs.

ABAC policies are built on a policy-based decision model, where each access request is evaluated against a set of rules defined in policies. These policies specify conditions that must be met before granting access. Instead of relying on static permissions, ABAC dynamically assesses attributes and applies logical expressions to determine access rights. This model enhances security by ensuring that access is granted only when all specified conditions align with the access control policy.

A typical ABAC policy consists of four key components:

Subjects – Entities requesting access, such as users, applications, devices, or automated processes.

Objects – Resources being accessed, such as files, databases, APIs, or applications.

Actions – The operations performed on objects, such as read, write, delete, or execute.

Conditions – Rules that define how attributes are evaluated to determine whether access should be granted or denied.

The flexibility of ABAC comes from its ability to define policy expressions using logical operators and attribute comparisons. Policies are often written in structured languages such as eXtensible Access

Control Markup Language (XACML), which provides a standardized way to express rules and enforce access control decisions.

For example, a basic ABAC policy expression could be:

"If the user's department is 'Finance' AND the requested action is 'Read' AND the resource classification is 'Confidential,' THEN allow access."

This policy checks three attributes—user department, action type, and resource classification—before granting access. If any condition is not met, access is denied.

ABAC policies can be categorized into different policy models, depending on the level of granularity and complexity required. Some common ABAC policy models include:

Identity-Based Policies

Identity-based policies evaluate attributes related to the subject's identity, such as username, job title, department, or security clearance. These policies ensure that access is granted only to authorized individuals based on their organizational role or identity attributes.

Example policy expression:

"If user.title = 'Manager' AND user.department = 'HR,' THEN allow access to employee records."

This ensures that only managers within the HR department can access employee records, preventing unauthorized access from users in other departments.

Resource-Based Policies

Resource-based policies focus on attributes of the object being accessed, such as data sensitivity, file ownership, or encryption level. These policies define access control rules based on the properties of the resource rather than the user.

Example policy expression:

"If document.classification = 'Public,' THEN allow access to all users."

This rule grants unrestricted access to publicly classified documents while maintaining stricter controls over confidential or sensitive resources.

Context-Aware Policies

Context-aware policies introduce environmental and situational factors into access control decisions. These policies evaluate attributes such as time of access, geographic location, device security posture, or network risk level.

Example policy expression:

"If user.location = 'Corporate Office' AND time.between(08:00, 18:00), THEN allow access to financial reports."

This policy ensures that financial reports can only be accessed from within the corporate office during business hours, adding an extra layer of security to prevent unauthorized access from external locations.

Risk-Based Policies

Risk-based policies incorporate security intelligence and behavioral analytics to determine access decisions dynamically. These policies assess risk factors such as login anomalies, failed authentication attempts, and behavioral deviations before granting or denying access.

Example policy expression:

"If user.failedLoginAttempts > 3 OR user.deviceCompliance = 'Non-Compliant,' THEN require multi-factor authentication (MFA) before granting access."

This ensures that users exhibiting suspicious behavior or using non-compliant devices are subject to additional authentication measures before gaining access.

Obligation-Based Policies

Obligation-based policies include actions that must be executed before or after granting access. These policies enforce additional requirements, such as logging access events, notifying administrators, or enforcing data encryption.

Example policy expression:

"If user.role = 'Data Analyst' AND document.sensitivity = 'Restricted,' THEN log access attempt AND notify compliance officer."

This ensures that access attempts to restricted data are logged and reported to compliance teams, improving security monitoring and accountability.

ABAC policy expressions use logical operators, mathematical comparisons, and rule sets to define access control decisions. Common logical operators used in ABAC policies include:

AND – All conditions must be met for access to be granted.

OR – At least one condition must be met for access to be granted.

NOT – Denies access if a specific condition is met.

EQUALS (=) – Checks if an attribute matches a specific value.

GREATER THAN / LESS THAN (>, <) – Compares numerical values, such as risk scores or time-based conditions.

IN LIST – Determines if an attribute value exists within a predefined list of acceptable values.

ABAC policy models and expressions provide organizations with a highly adaptable and scalable approach to access control. By combining identity-based, resource-based, context-aware, risk-based, and obligation-based policies, organizations can create access control frameworks that meet diverse security and compliance requirements. The ability to evaluate multiple attributes in real-time ensures that access decisions remain aligned with organizational policies while adapting to changing risk conditions.

Implementing ABAC policies requires careful planning, attribute management, and integration with identity and access management (IAM) solutions. Organizations should define meaningful attributes, establish clear policy rules, and leverage policy enforcement mechanisms such as Policy Decision Points (PDP) and Policy Enforcement Points (PEP) to apply ABAC controls consistently. By utilizing structured policy expressions and standardized languages like XACML, organizations can enforce dynamic, fine-grained access control policies that enhance security, improve compliance, and support evolving IT environments.

Dynamic Authorization with ABAC

Dynamic authorization is one of the most powerful capabilities of Attribute-Based Access Control (ABAC), allowing organizations to enforce real-time, context-aware access control policies. Unlike static access control models such as Role-Based Access Control (RBAC), which rely on predefined role assignments, ABAC evaluates multiple attributes dynamically to determine access rights. This approach ensures that access decisions reflect the latest user attributes, environmental conditions, and security context, making it particularly valuable for modern IT environments that require agility and adaptability.

At the core of dynamic authorization in ABAC is the ability to make access decisions based on real-time attributes rather than fixed permissions. In traditional models, access rights are assigned once and do not change unless an administrator updates them. However, in dynamic environments such as cloud computing, remote work, and digital applications, user attributes, device status, and security risks change frequently. Dynamic authorization enables organizations to respond to these changes instantly, ensuring that access remains appropriate at all times.

A key advantage of dynamic authorization is context-aware access control. ABAC policies evaluate contextual factors such as user location, time of access, device security posture, network risk level, and authentication strength. These attributes provide an additional layer of security by allowing or denying access based on situational awareness. For example, a policy could allow a user to access a financial application only if they are connecting from a corporate office using a company-approved device. If the same user attempts to access the application from an untrusted network, the policy may enforce additional authentication steps or deny access altogether.

Dynamic authorization also supports risk-based access control by integrating real-time risk assessments into access decisions. Organizations can use risk scores, behavioral analytics, and anomaly detection to determine whether an access request should be granted, denied, or require additional authentication. For example, if a user logs in from an unusual geographic location or outside their normal working hours, an ABAC system can detect this anomaly and enforce step-up authentication before granting access. This adaptive approach reduces the risk of compromised credentials being used for unauthorized access.

Another critical component of dynamic authorization is just-in-time (JIT) access, which grants permissions only when needed and for a limited time. Unlike traditional models where users retain access permanently based on role assignments, JIT access ensures that privileges are activated only when a specific condition is met. This is particularly useful in privileged access management (PAM) scenarios, where administrative users require elevated permissions temporarily to perform a task. By enforcing time-limited access, organizations reduce the risk of long-term privilege accumulation and insider threats.

Policy decision and enforcement mechanisms play a crucial role in enabling dynamic authorization in ABAC. The system relies on two primary components:

Policy Decision Point (PDP) – The PDP is responsible for evaluating access requests in real time. It retrieves relevant attributes, applies predefined access policies, and makes a decision to allow or deny access. The PDP considers multiple attributes dynamically, ensuring that each request is evaluated against the latest data.

Policy Enforcement Point (PEP) – The PEP intercepts access requests and enforces the decision made by the PDP. If access is granted, the PEP allows the request to proceed. If access is denied, the PEP blocks the request and may trigger additional security actions, such as logging the event or notifying administrators.

The interaction between PDP and PEP ensures that access control decisions are both dynamic and consistent across an organization's infrastructure. By integrating with identity and access management (IAM) solutions, ABAC policies can be enforced across cloud services, on-premises applications, and hybrid environments.

Dynamic authorization also enhances compliance and regulatory adherence by ensuring that access control policies are enforced in real time based on compliance requirements. Many regulations, such as GDPR, HIPAA, and PCI DSS, mandate strict access control measures to protect sensitive data. ABAC enables organizations to enforce fine-grained access policies that adapt to changing compliance conditions. For instance, a healthcare provider may enforce a policy that allows doctors to access patient records only during their working hours and only when treating assigned patients. If a doctor attempts to access records outside these conditions, the system can block access and generate an audit log for compliance reporting.

Organizations implementing dynamic authorization with ABAC must focus on attribute management and governance to ensure accuracy and consistency. Attributes must be sourced from reliable systems such as HR databases, directory services, endpoint security platforms, and identity providers. Without proper attribute governance, outdated or incorrect attribute values could lead to improper access decisions. Organizations should establish attribute validation processes and automate attribute synchronization to maintain data integrity.

One of the biggest advantages of ABAC's dynamic authorization is fine-grained access control. Unlike RBAC, which assigns broad permissions based on roles, ABAC can define precise access conditions based on specific attribute values. For example, instead of granting all engineers access to a development environment, a dynamic ABAC policy can restrict access to engineers who are assigned to a particular project, using a specific device, and working from an approved location. This level of granularity significantly reduces the risk of unauthorized access while maintaining operational efficiency.

Organizations can further enhance dynamic authorization by leveraging machine learning and artificial intelligence (AI) for real-time policy enforcement. AI-driven ABAC systems can analyze historical access patterns, detect anomalies, and adjust policies dynamically based on emerging threats. For example, if an AI model detects an unusual spike in access requests from a particular department, it can trigger an automatic review of access policies and recommend adjustments to mitigate potential security risks. This proactive approach strengthens security posture by adapting to evolving threats.

Integration with Zero Trust security models is another key benefit of dynamic authorization. Zero Trust principles require continuous verification of user identity, device health, and contextual risk before granting access. ABAC aligns with this model by enforcing policies that verify attributes dynamically at every access request. This ensures that users do not receive implicit trust based on prior authentication but must continuously meet security conditions to maintain access.

To successfully implement dynamic authorization with ABAC, organizations should adopt best practices such as:

Defining clear access control policies that incorporate multiple attributes and contextual factors.

Automating attribute management to ensure that real-time data is accurate and up to date.

Integrating with security monitoring tools to detect and respond to suspicious access attempts.

Conducting regular access reviews to ensure policies remain aligned with business and security requirements.

Testing and refining policies using simulation tools to evaluate access scenarios before deployment.

Dynamic authorization with ABAC provides a scalable, flexible, and security-enhanced approach to access control. By leveraging real-time attribute evaluation, risk-based access decisions, and continuous verification, organizations can protect sensitive resources, reduce security risks, and improve compliance. This adaptive security model ensures that access control policies remain effective in rapidly changing IT environments, making ABAC a critical component of modern identity and access management strategies.

Attribute Management and Governance

Attribute-Based Access Control (ABAC) relies on attributes to determine access rights dynamically, making attribute management and governance essential for a successful implementation. Attributes serve as the foundation for policy enforcement, allowing organizations to define access rules based on user identity, resource characteristics, actions, and contextual factors. Without proper governance, attribute data can become outdated, inconsistent, or unreliable, leading to security gaps and improper access decisions. Effective attribute management ensures that access control policies remain accurate, scalable, and compliant with security and regulatory requirements.

The first step in attribute management is defining a structured attribute taxonomy that categorizes and standardizes the attributes used in access control policies. Attributes should be classified into four main categories:

Subject Attributes – These describe the user or entity requesting access, including job title, department, role, security clearance, device type, authentication method, and risk score.

Object Attributes – These define properties of the resource being accessed, such as document classification, data sensitivity level, ownership, and encryption status.

Action Attributes – These specify the type of operation being performed on the resource, such as read, write, modify, delete, or execute.

Environmental Attributes – These include contextual factors such as time of access, geographic location, network security level, device compliance status, and threat intelligence data.

By organizing attributes into these categories, organizations can ensure that access control policies remain clear and consistent. A well-structured attribute taxonomy simplifies policy development, improves policy accuracy, and enhances security by enabling fine-grained access decisions.

Attribute governance involves establishing rules, policies, and procedures to manage the lifecycle of attributes. This includes defining how attributes are created, updated, stored, and retired. Organizations must determine which systems serve as the authoritative source for attribute data, ensuring that attributes are derived from reliable sources such as HR databases, directory services (e.g., Active Directory, LDAP), security monitoring tools, and identity providers.

A critical aspect of attribute governance is attribute validation and accuracy. Since access control decisions depend on real-time attribute evaluations, organizations must implement processes to ensure that attribute values are accurate and up to date. Outdated or incorrect attributes can lead to improper access grants or denials, increasing security risks. Automated synchronization between identity management systems and access control platforms helps maintain attribute integrity. Regular audits should be conducted to detect inconsistencies and correct inaccurate attribute data.

Attribute lifecycle management ensures that attributes remain relevant and effective throughout their lifecycle. Attributes should be periodically reviewed to determine whether they are still necessary and whether they accurately reflect the current state of users, resources, and environments. Lifecycle management involves:

Attribute creation – Defining new attributes based on business requirements and security policies.

Attribute updates – Ensuring that attributes are modified in response to organizational changes, such as job promotions, role transitions, and department restructuring.

Attribute expiration and decommissioning – Removing attributes that are no longer relevant to prevent security risks and maintain data hygiene.

Automating attribute lifecycle management reduces administrative overhead and improves the accuracy of access control policies. Identity governance and administration (IGA) tools help organizations manage attribute updates efficiently by integrating with HR systems, monitoring access patterns, and triggering updates based on real-time events.

One of the challenges in attribute management is attribute consistency across multiple systems. Organizations often operate in hybrid environments, where attributes are stored across on-premises and cloud-based systems. If attribute definitions vary between systems, policy inconsistencies can arise, leading to access control failures. Standardizing attribute definitions and formats across all platforms ensures that attributes are interpreted correctly during policy evaluations. Organizations should establish governance frameworks that define attribute naming conventions, acceptable values, and synchronization mechanisms.

Security and privacy considerations are also essential when managing attributes. Since attributes often contain sensitive information, organizations must implement data protection measures to prevent unauthorized access or misuse. Role-based access control (RBAC) can be applied to attribute management itself, ensuring that only authorized personnel can modify or view attribute data. Additionally, encryption, anonymization, and access logging should be used to safeguard sensitive attributes such as personally identifiable information (PII), security clearance levels, and financial classifications.

Attribute quality and completeness play a significant role in ABAC effectiveness. Missing or incomplete attribute data can lead to policy misfires, where legitimate users are denied access or unauthorized users gain access due to missing constraints. Organizations should implement data validation checks to ensure that all necessary attributes are populated and that no access decisions are made based on incomplete information. AI-driven anomaly detection tools can also help identify discrepancies in attribute data and suggest corrective actions.

Governance policies should define attribute ownership and accountability. Each attribute should have a designated owner responsible for maintaining its accuracy and ensuring that updates are applied as needed. Attribute owners may be HR personnel, IT administrators, or security teams, depending on the type of attribute. By assigning ownership, organizations create accountability structures that enhance attribute reliability and compliance with access control policies.

To maintain compliance with regulatory requirements such as GDPR, HIPAA, and SOX, organizations must enforce attribute governance audits. These audits assess whether attribute data is being managed according to policy requirements, whether attribute-based policies align with compliance frameworks, and whether sensitive attributes are being protected appropriately. Audit reports help organizations identify gaps in attribute management and take corrective actions to strengthen security and compliance.

Organizations implementing ABAC should also consider attribute federation and interoperability when integrating with external systems and third-party services. In federated identity environments, attributes must be exchanged between identity providers and service providers to enable seamless access control across multiple organizations or cloud platforms. Standard protocols such as Security Assertion Markup Language (SAML) and OpenID Connect (OIDC) facilitate secure attribute sharing, ensuring that federated access control policies are enforced consistently.

To improve operational efficiency, organizations can leverage machine learning and AI-driven automation for attribute management. AI can analyze historical access patterns to suggest attribute refinements, detect anomalies in attribute data, and automate attribute updates based on risk assessments. For example, an AI-based system can flag employees who have excessive access based on attribute mismatches and recommend policy adjustments. By integrating AI into attribute governance, organizations can enhance security posture and reduce administrative effort.

Training and awareness are also essential in attribute management and governance. Employees and administrators should understand the role of attributes in access control and the importance of maintaining attribute accuracy. Security teams should educate personnel on best practices for attribute updates, data classification, and compliance with attribute governance policies. Well-informed teams contribute to a more secure and reliable ABAC implementation.

Effective attribute management and governance form the backbone of a strong ABAC implementation. By ensuring that attributes are accurate, consistently applied, and properly governed, organizations can maintain dynamic and context-aware access control policies that enhance security, reduce administrative overhead, and support regulatory compliance. With the right governance frameworks, automation tools, and security controls in place, attribute management can become a seamless and scalable component of enterprise security strategies.

Context-Aware Access Control with ABAC

Context-aware access control is a fundamental aspect of Attribute-Based Access Control (ABAC), allowing organizations to enforce dynamic security policies that adapt to changing conditions. Unlike static access control models, which rely solely on predefined roles or group memberships, ABAC evaluates multiple attributes in real time to determine whether access should be granted or denied. This approach enhances security by considering contextual factors such as user location, device security posture, time of access, and network conditions. By leveraging context-aware policies, organizations can implement more granular and risk-based access control mechanisms that better protect sensitive data and systems.

A key advantage of context-aware access control in ABAC is the ability to enforce adaptive security policies that respond to real-time conditions. Traditional access control models often grant users broad permissions that remain unchanged unless manually updated by administrators. In contrast, ABAC allows organizations to define policies that adjust access rights dynamically based on context. For example, an employee working from a corporate office may have unrestricted access to a cloud-based document management system, while the same employee attempting to access the system from an untrusted public Wi-Fi network may be required to complete multi-factor authentication (MFA) before gaining access.

One of the most important contextual attributes in ABAC is geolocation. Organizations can use geolocation data to enforce access policies that restrict access based on geographic regions. For example, an organization might allow employees to access customer data only when they are within an approved geographic zone, such as their home country. If an access attempt originates from a high-risk region known for cyber threats, the system can block access or require additional authentication. Geolocation-based access control helps prevent unauthorized access from foreign actors attempting to compromise user credentials.

Time-based access control is another powerful context-aware security measure in ABAC. Organizations can define policies that grant access only during specific time windows, reducing the risk of unauthorized after-hours access. For example, an enterprise might restrict access to financial systems to business hours, ensuring that employees cannot perform financial transactions outside of approved working hours. Additionally, organizations can implement time-sensitive access policies for temporary access, allowing users to access certain resources only for a limited period before their permissions automatically expire.

Device security posture is another critical contextual factor that influences access decisions in ABAC. Organizations can define policies that evaluate whether a user's device meets security requirements before granting access. For example, a policy may allow access to corporate applications only if the user's device has the latest security updates installed, an active firewall, and is free of known malware infections. If a device does not meet security compliance requirements, access can be restricted, or the user may be redirected to a remediation process. This approach helps mitigate risks associated with compromised or non-compliant endpoints.

ABAC also supports network-based access control, allowing organizations to assess the security level of the network from which access requests originate. Policies can differentiate between secure corporate networks, home office networks, and public or high-risk networks. For example, an employee accessing corporate resources from an internal office network may receive full access privileges, while the same employee accessing from a coffee shop's public Wi-Fi may be restricted to read-only access or required to use a virtual private network (VPN) before proceeding. This contextual awareness helps organizations enforce security policies that minimize the risk of data breaches caused by unsecured network connections.

Another significant benefit of context-aware access control is risk-based authentication and authorization. Organizations can integrate risk engines that analyze multiple contextual attributes to assess the likelihood of an access request being fraudulent. Factors such as login history, behavioral patterns, and device reputation can be used to calculate a risk score. If a login attempt deviates from normal behavior—such as an unusual IP address, an unrecognized device, or an atypical login time—the system can enforce additional security measures such as step-up authentication or temporary access restrictions.

Context-aware access control also enhances zero trust security architectures, where continuous verification is required before granting or maintaining access. Zero trust principles dictate that access should never be assumed based on prior authentication alone. Instead, every access request must be evaluated dynamically based on current contextual factors. ABAC aligns with zero trust by ensuring that access decisions are continuously reassessed based on the latest attribute data, reducing the risk of unauthorized lateral movement within networks.

Organizations implementing context-aware access control with ABAC must establish reliable attribute sources to ensure that access decisions are based on accurate and up-to-date information. Attributes such as device health status, geolocation, and network security level should be sourced from trusted identity and security management systems. Automating attribute collection and synchronization ensures that access policies remain effective without requiring manual intervention.

One of the challenges in implementing context-aware access control is balancing security with usability. Overly restrictive policies can frustrate users and hinder productivity, while overly permissive policies can expose organizations to security risks. To address this challenge, organizations should adopt adaptive access control models that adjust access restrictions dynamically based on risk assessments. For example, low-risk scenarios (such as an employee logging in from a trusted device within an approved office location) may allow seamless access, while higher-risk scenarios (such as an employee logging in from an unknown device in an unfamiliar location) may trigger stricter security controls.

Organizations should also integrate policy enforcement mechanisms that operate at multiple levels of the IT environment. Policy enforcement points (PEPs) should be deployed across identity providers, cloud applications, enterprise networks, and endpoint security solutions to ensure that context-aware access controls are applied consistently. By integrating with security information and event management (SIEM) systems, organizations can monitor access control events, detect anomalies, and fine-tune policies based on emerging security threats.

Regular policy reviews and updates are necessary to ensure that context-aware access control policies remain effective. As business requirements, threat landscapes, and technology infrastructures evolve, organizations must continuously assess and refine their ABAC policies. Conducting access control audits and reviewing contextual attributes ensures that policies remain aligned with security and compliance objectives.

Context-aware access control with ABAC provides organizations with a scalable and adaptive security framework that enhances protection against unauthorized access, insider threats, and cyberattacks. By leveraging real-time attributes such as geolocation, device security posture, network conditions, and behavioral analytics, organizations can enforce security policies that dynamically adjust to changing risks. This approach strengthens security posture while ensuring that legitimate users can access resources efficiently without unnecessary friction. With the increasing complexity of IT environments and the growing sophistication of cyber threats, context-aware ABAC is a critical component of modern access control strategies.

ABAC in Microservices and API Security

Attribute-Based Access Control (ABAC) has become a critical component of securing modern microservices and APIs, providing fine-grained access control that dynamically evaluates multiple attributes before granting access. Unlike traditional access control models, ABAC enables organizations to enforce security policies that consider user attributes, request context, resource sensitivity, and environmental conditions. In distributed architectures such as microservices and API-driven applications, ABAC enhances security by ensuring that each request is evaluated dynamically based on real-time data, reducing security risks while maintaining operational flexibility.

Microservices architectures decompose applications into smaller, loosely coupled services that communicate with each other through APIs. This approach improves scalability, maintainability, and agility but introduces new security challenges. Traditional access control models such as Role-Based Access Control (RBAC) are often insufficient for microservices environments because they rely on predefined roles that do not account for dynamic conditions. ABAC, on the other hand, allows organizations to define policies that adapt to contextual factors such as API request parameters, user identity, time of request, location, and device security posture.

One of the primary advantages of ABAC in microservices security is its ability to enforce fine-grained authorization at the API level. Each microservice can define its own access policies based on a combination of attributes rather than relying on static role assignments. For example, an ABAC policy could allow an API request to retrieve customer data only if the requestor has a "customer_support" attribute and the request originates from a corporate IP address. If the same request is made from an external network, access could be denied or require additional authentication.

API security is another area where ABAC plays a crucial role by securing endpoints against unauthorized access. APIs are the primary communication channels between microservices, making them frequent targets for attacks such as API abuse, unauthorized data extraction, and privilege escalation. ABAC ensures that every API request is evaluated based on predefined policies before processing. By integrating ABAC with API gateways, organizations can enforce access control policies consistently across all API endpoints, reducing the risk of unauthorized access.

One of the key components in securing APIs with ABAC is the Policy Enforcement Point (PEP), which intercepts API requests and enforces access control decisions based on attribute evaluation. The PEP queries a Policy Decision Point (PDP) to determine whether a request should be allowed, denied, or require additional authentication. The PDP applies predefined policies that evaluate multiple attributes, including:

User attributes – Identity, role, department, authentication strength, risk score.

Resource attributes – API endpoint classification, data sensitivity, ownership, encryption status.

Action attributes – HTTP method (GET, POST, DELETE, PUT), type of operation requested.

Contextual attributes – Request source IP, device compliance, geolocation, time of access.

For example, an API handling financial transactions may define an ABAC policy such as:

"Allow transactions only if the user has a 'Finance_Officer' attribute, the transaction amount is less than $10,000, and the request originates from a company-managed device."

By enforcing these dynamic conditions, ABAC prevents unauthorized transactions while allowing legitimate requests to proceed without unnecessary restrictions.

Dynamic authorization in API security is particularly useful for handling external integrations and third-party access. Many organizations expose APIs to partners, vendors, and customers, requiring access controls that extend beyond internal user roles. ABAC enables organizations to grant access based on business relationships, contractual agreements, and security requirements. For instance, a partner API client may be allowed to retrieve limited customer data based on its "partner_tier" attribute, while an internal API client may have broader access.

In microservices environments, ABAC also helps mitigate the over-permissioning problem, where users and applications receive excessive access privileges due to static role assignments. Instead of granting broad API permissions based on user roles, ABAC evaluates each request based on real-time attributes. This minimizes security risks by ensuring that API consumers only access the data and operations necessary for their specific use case.

Another important use case for ABAC in microservices security is multi-tenancy enforcement. Many cloud-native applications serve multiple customers (tenants) within the same infrastructure, requiring strict isolation between tenant data. ABAC policies can enforce tenant-based access control by ensuring that API requests include valid tenant identifiers and that users can only access resources belonging to their assigned tenant.

For example, an ABAC policy for a multi-tenant application might enforce:

"Allow data access if the requestor's 'tenant_id' attribute matches the resource's 'owner_tenant_id' attribute."

This prevents unauthorized cross-tenant data access, ensuring data privacy and compliance with regulatory requirements.

API security frameworks such as OAuth 2.0 and OpenID Connect (OIDC) can be integrated with ABAC to strengthen API authentication and authorization. While OAuth handles secure token-based authentication, ABAC evaluates request attributes to enforce fine-grained authorization policies. This combination enhances security by ensuring that even authenticated users must meet additional attribute-based conditions before accessing sensitive API endpoints.

Another critical aspect of ABAC in microservices security is policy versioning and auditing. Access control policies should be versioned and logged to provide visibility into access decisions and enable auditability. If a security incident occurs, organizations need to trace which API requests were allowed or denied based on historical policies. Logging and monitoring ABAC decisions help organizations identify unauthorized access attempts, detect policy misconfigurations, and maintain compliance with industry regulations.

Implementing ABAC in microservices and API security requires careful attribute management and synchronization. Since ABAC relies on real-time attribute evaluation, organizations must ensure that attributes are accurately maintained across identity providers, security monitoring tools, and API management platforms. Attributes should be synchronized dynamically to prevent stale data from influencing access control decisions.

Organizations can further enhance API security by integrating ABAC with runtime security monitoring and anomaly detection. AI-powered security analytics can analyze API request patterns to identify suspicious behavior, such as abnormal data access volumes or API scraping attempts. ABAC policies can be extended to include risk-based adaptive access controls, where high-risk API requests trigger additional verification steps before proceeding.

Adopting ABAC for microservices and API security provides organizations with a scalable, flexible, and adaptive approach to access control. Unlike static models, ABAC continuously evaluates multiple attributes in real-time, enabling organizations to enforce granular security policies that adapt to evolving threats and business requirements. By integrating ABAC with API gateways, identity providers, and security monitoring tools, organizations can build robust access control frameworks that protect sensitive data, prevent unauthorized access, and ensure compliance in distributed environments.

Challenges in Implementing ABAC at Scale

Implementing Attribute-Based Access Control (ABAC) at scale presents significant challenges due to the complexity of attribute management, policy enforcement, system integration, and performance considerations. While ABAC offers a highly flexible and dynamic approach to access control, large-scale deployments require careful planning to avoid inefficiencies, security gaps, and administrative overhead. Organizations that attempt to implement ABAC without a clear strategy may struggle with policy management, attribute inconsistencies, and system performance degradation. Understanding these challenges is essential to successfully deploying ABAC in enterprise environments.

One of the most significant challenges in large-scale ABAC implementations is attribute management and governance. ABAC relies on attributes to make access control decisions, meaning that organizations must maintain accurate, up-to-date attribute data across multiple systems. In a large enterprise, attributes such as user roles, job functions, device status, and security classifications may be stored in different databases, identity providers, and application platforms. Synchronizing and normalizing these attributes across all systems is complex, requiring automated workflows and data governance policies. Without proper attribute management, ABAC policies may rely on stale or incorrect data, leading to unauthorized access or improper denials.

Another major challenge is policy complexity and scalability. ABAC policies can be highly granular, incorporating multiple attributes, conditions, and contextual factors. As an organization grows, the number of policies required to cover various access scenarios increases exponentially. Unlike Role-Based Access Control (RBAC), where administrators manage a predefined set of roles, ABAC policies must account for dynamic attributes that change over time. Managing thousands of policies across multiple systems can quickly become overwhelming without an efficient policy lifecycle management process. Organizations must establish a centralized policy repository, implement policy versioning, and automate policy updates to prevent inconsistencies and policy sprawl.

Performance and latency issues also pose significant challenges in large-scale ABAC implementations. Because ABAC evaluates multiple attributes dynamically for each access request, policy decision engines must process a vast amount of data in real time. In high-volume environments, such as cloud platforms, banking systems, or e-commerce applications, slow policy evaluations can impact user experience and system performance. To mitigate this issue, organizations must optimize their Policy Decision Points (PDPs) by implementing caching mechanisms, distributed policy evaluation, and indexing strategies that reduce processing time. Additionally, integrating ABAC with existing identity and access management (IAM) solutions should be done in a way that minimizes latency without compromising security.

Integration with legacy systems is another critical challenge. Many large enterprises operate a mix of modern cloud-based applications and older on-premises systems that were not designed to support ABAC. Legacy systems often use traditional RBAC models or even discretionary access control (DAC), making it difficult to enforce attribute-based policies. Retrofitting ABAC into these systems may require significant modifications, such as developing middleware layers that translate ABAC policies into role-based or rule-based decisions. In some cases, organizations may need to adopt a hybrid access control model, combining RBAC for legacy applications and ABAC for modern services.

Ensuring consistent policy enforcement across multiple environments is also a complex task. Organizations that operate in hybrid or multi-cloud environments must ensure that ABAC policies are applied consistently across all platforms. Cloud providers such as AWS, Microsoft Azure, and Google Cloud each have their own IAM frameworks, making it challenging to implement unified ABAC policies across different infrastructures. Enterprises must develop a federated access control strategy that centralizes policy enforcement while allowing local adjustments to meet specific cloud security requirements. Without a unified approach, discrepancies in policy enforcement may lead to security gaps or compliance violations.

Another challenge in scaling ABAC is balancing security with usability. Highly restrictive ABAC policies can frustrate users and hinder productivity, while overly permissive policies can expose the organization to security risks. Organizations must continuously refine policies to strike the right balance between security and operational efficiency. One way to achieve this is by implementing risk-based adaptive access control, where ABAC policies dynamically adjust based on real-time risk assessments. For example, a system might allow full access to a sensitive document if the request comes from an office workstation but require additional authentication if accessed from an external location. This approach ensures security without unnecessarily restricting legitimate access.

Auditing and compliance requirements further complicate large-scale ABAC deployments. Many regulatory frameworks, such as GDPR, HIPAA, and SOX, require organizations to track and report access control decisions. Unlike RBAC, where access is granted based on predefined roles, ABAC dynamically evaluates attributes, making it more difficult to maintain clear audit logs. Organizations must implement comprehensive logging and monitoring mechanisms that capture attribute values, policy evaluations, and access decisions in a structured format. Security teams must also develop reporting tools that allow auditors to review access patterns and policy changes over time.

Policy conflicts and rule resolution present another significant challenge in ABAC. As organizations expand their use of ABAC, different teams may define overlapping or conflicting policies. For example, a policy allowing remote employees to access certain systems may contradict another policy restricting access based on network security conditions. Organizations must establish a clear policy conflict resolution framework that defines precedence rules and mechanisms for handling conflicting policies. Automated policy validation tools can help detect and resolve inconsistencies before policies are enforced.

Another obstacle in large-scale ABAC implementations is user and administrator training. Because ABAC policies rely on complex attribute evaluations rather than simple role assignments, security teams, IT administrators, and business stakeholders must understand how to define and manage policies effectively. Organizations should invest in policy modeling tools, training programs, and simulation environments where administrators can test policies before deploying them in production. Without proper training, misconfigured ABAC policies may lead to excessive access privileges or unintended access denials.

Lastly, adoption resistance and cultural challenges can hinder ABAC implementation at scale. Many organizations have long relied on RBAC and may be hesitant to transition to a more complex access control model. Business units may resist changes that alter existing workflows, fearing that ABAC will introduce operational disruptions. To overcome these challenges, organizations must take a gradual approach to ABAC adoption, starting with high-risk use cases and expanding implementation over time. Engaging key stakeholders early in the process and demonstrating ABAC's benefits—such as improved security, reduced administrative overhead, and enhanced compliance—can help gain executive and employee support.

Successfully implementing ABAC at scale requires a combination of technology, governance, automation, and organizational change management. By addressing challenges related to attribute management, policy complexity, system performance, integration with legacy applications, and compliance, organizations can develop a scalable ABAC framework that enhances security without compromising efficiency. Large-scale ABAC deployments demand careful planning, continuous monitoring, and iterative improvements to ensure that policies remain effective in rapidly evolving IT environments. Organizations that overcome these challenges will benefit from a dynamic, flexible, and future-proof access control model that strengthens security while supporting business agility.

ABAC and Artificial Intelligence: The Future of Access Control

As organizations move towards more dynamic and complex IT environments, traditional access control models struggle to keep up with evolving security demands. Attribute-Based Access Control (ABAC) has emerged as a flexible and scalable solution, allowing access decisions to be based on multiple attributes and contextual factors. However, the increasing volume of access requests, attributes, and security conditions requires automation and intelligence beyond human capabilities. Artificial Intelligence (AI) is playing a transformative role in enhancing ABAC, making access control more adaptive, predictive, and efficient. By integrating AI with ABAC, organizations can improve security, automate decision-making, and proactively address emerging threats.

One of the key benefits of AI in ABAC is automated policy generation and optimization. Traditionally, security administrators must manually define and manage ABAC policies, which can be complex and time-consuming. AI-driven systems can analyze historical access patterns, user behavior, and risk assessments to suggest or generate access control policies automatically. Machine learning (ML) models can identify common access patterns across different user groups and recommend optimized policies that balance security with operational efficiency. For example, if AI detects that employees in a specific department consistently access certain resources under specific conditions, it can propose an access policy that aligns with these real-world behaviors while minimizing security risks.

AI also enhances ABAC by enabling dynamic and risk-based access control. Traditional access control policies often follow static rules that do not account for evolving security threats. AI-powered ABAC can evaluate real-time risk factors, such as unusual login behavior, device anomalies, and external threat intelligence, to make context-aware access decisions. For instance, if an employee attempts to access sensitive data from an unfamiliar location using an untrusted device, an AI-enhanced ABAC system can either block access, require additional authentication, or limit access privileges based on risk assessment. This dynamic approach reduces the risk of unauthorized access while allowing legitimate users to continue working without unnecessary friction.

Another major contribution of AI to ABAC is anomaly detection and behavioral analysis. AI can continuously monitor user behavior and detect deviations from normal patterns that may indicate potential security threats. For example, if an employee suddenly starts accessing systems that are outside their usual work scope or attempts to download large volumes of sensitive data, AI can flag this behavior as suspicious and trigger immediate security actions. By integrating AI with ABAC, organizations can respond to threats proactively, adjusting access permissions in real time based on detected anomalies.

AI-driven role and attribute discovery is another area where artificial intelligence enhances ABAC. In many organizations, attributes used for access control are often scattered across multiple identity providers, HR databases, and security tools. AI can analyze organizational data to discover and classify meaningful attributes that should be used in access control policies. This automation helps security teams define more accurate and relevant access policies without relying on manual attribute mapping. For example, AI can analyze email communication patterns, project assignments, and collaboration data to infer user roles and responsibilities dynamically, allowing for more granular and context-aware access control decisions.

The integration of AI with ABAC also improves incident response and remediation. When a security incident occurs, AI can automatically assess the impact of compromised credentials, insider threats, or privilege misuse. Instead of relying on manual security investigations, AI-driven ABAC can adjust access controls dynamically, isolating affected users, restricting high-risk transactions, and notifying security teams. This automated response mechanism helps contain security incidents before they escalate, minimizing potential damage to an organization's systems and data.

AI also enhances ABAC in multi-cloud and hybrid environments, where enforcing consistent access policies across different platforms can be challenging. Many enterprises use multiple cloud providers, each with its own access control mechanisms and attribute definitions. AI-powered ABAC solutions can unify and standardize access policies across cloud and on-premises environments, automatically mapping attributes and enforcing policies in a consistent manner. This eliminates the need for security teams to manually configure access control rules for each cloud provider, reducing complexity and improving security posture.

Explainable AI (XAI) in ABAC is another emerging trend that helps improve transparency and trust in AI-driven access control decisions. One of the concerns with AI-based security solutions is the "black box" problem, where AI models make decisions without clear explanations. In ABAC, explainable AI ensures that access control decisions are interpretable, providing security administrators with insights into why access was granted or denied. This transparency is crucial for compliance, auditability, and policy refinement, allowing organizations to fine-tune their ABAC policies based on AI-generated insights.

Another area where AI is transforming ABAC is predictive access control, which leverages machine learning to anticipate future access needs. By analyzing historical access patterns, AI can predict which resources an employee is likely to require based on their job role, project involvement, or past behavior. Instead of waiting for access requests to be manually approved, predictive ABAC can proactively grant access to resources that users are expected to need, reducing administrative delays while maintaining security controls. This approach is particularly useful in large enterprises with dynamic work environments, where employees frequently move between teams and require temporary access to different systems.

AI-powered ABAC is also playing a crucial role in regulatory compliance and audit automation. Many industries require organizations to enforce strict access control policies to comply with regulations such as GDPR, HIPAA, and SOX. AI can assist with compliance by automatically generating audit reports, identifying access violations, and recommending corrective actions. By continuously monitoring access policies and user behavior, AI ensures that organizations remain compliant with regulatory requirements without the need for manual audits.

The future of access control will see AI and ABAC working together to create self-adaptive security frameworks. Instead of static access control policies that require constant human intervention, AI-driven ABAC systems will continuously learn from real-world access patterns, security incidents, and business requirements to refine and optimize policies automatically. Organizations that adopt AI-powered ABAC will benefit from enhanced security, reduced administrative overhead, and improved agility in managing access control across complex IT ecosystems.

As cyber threats become more sophisticated and IT environments continue to evolve, AI-driven ABAC will become a critical component of modern security architectures. By leveraging machine learning, behavioral analytics, and predictive modeling, organizations can implement access control policies that dynamically adapt to changing risk conditions while ensuring compliance and operational efficiency. AI-enhanced ABAC represents the next generation of access control, providing a scalable and intelligent security framework that meets the demands of an increasingly interconnected digital world.

ABAC Use Cases in Government and Healthcare

Attribute-Based Access Control (ABAC) has become a critical security model for organizations that require dynamic, fine-grained access control. In sectors such as government and healthcare, where data sensitivity, regulatory compliance, and security threats are key concerns, ABAC provides the flexibility needed to enforce strict access policies while maintaining operational efficiency. By leveraging attributes such as user identity, role, location, device security posture, and contextual conditions, ABAC enables real-time access decisions that align with security policies and legal requirements.

In government agencies, ABAC is widely used to enforce classified access policies, ensuring that sensitive information is only accessible to authorized personnel under specific conditions. Traditional access control models such as Role-Based Access Control (RBAC) are often too rigid to accommodate the complex requirements of government systems, which must consider factors such as security clearance levels, mission roles, and geopolitical conditions. ABAC allows agencies to define access policies that adapt dynamically based on changing security risks.

For example, a government intelligence agency may implement an ABAC policy that allows analysts to access classified documents only if they hold the appropriate security clearance and are working from a secure facility. If an analyst attempts to access the same document from an untrusted network or outside of designated work hours, ABAC can either deny access or require additional authentication steps. This ensures that sensitive government data remains protected while allowing authorized personnel to perform their duties under secure conditions.

Another critical ABAC use case in government is inter-agency collaboration. Government agencies frequently share data and resources with other departments, law enforcement entities, and international partners. ABAC facilitates secure data sharing by defining policies that restrict access based on organizational affiliation, case-specific criteria, and legal jurisdiction. For instance, a policy might allow federal law enforcement officers to access a suspect's case file only if they are assigned to an active investigation and have obtained proper authorization. This level of granularity prevents overexposure of sensitive information while enabling necessary collaboration.

ABAC also enhances security for government contractors and third-party access. Many government agencies rely on external vendors, consultants, and contractors who require temporary access to specific resources. ABAC enables agencies to grant time-limited and purpose-specific access based on contract details, project roles, and compliance status. A defense contractor working on a classified project, for example, may be granted access to design documents only during the contract period and only from approved devices with up-to-date security configurations. Once the contract expires, ABAC automatically revokes access, reducing the risk of data leaks.

In the healthcare sector, ABAC plays a crucial role in protecting patient data while ensuring that medical professionals have timely access to the information they need. Healthcare environments require strict access controls due to compliance regulations such as the Health Insurance Portability and Accountability Act (HIPAA) and the General Data Protection Regulation (GDPR). Traditional role-based access models often struggle to balance security with the dynamic nature of patient care, where doctors, nurses, and specialists need different levels of access based on their responsibilities.

One of the most important ABAC use cases in healthcare is electronic health record (EHR) access control. ABAC allows hospitals and clinics to define access policies that ensure patient data is only available to authorized personnel based on contextual factors. A policy might allow a primary care physician to view and update a patient's medical history but restrict access to mental health records unless the physician is actively treating the patient. Similarly, a nurse may be permitted to update a patient's medication schedule but not access financial or billing information.

ABAC also improves emergency access management in healthcare. During medical emergencies, healthcare professionals may need immediate access to patient records, even if they do not normally have the required permissions. ABAC enables break-glass access policies, which temporarily grant emergency access under controlled conditions. For instance, if a trauma surgeon needs access to a patient's restricted medical records during a life-threatening situation, ABAC can allow access while logging the event and notifying compliance officers for post-incident review. This ensures that patient safety is prioritized without compromising security and auditability.

Another key ABAC application in healthcare is telemedicine and remote patient monitoring. With the rise of digital health services, medical professionals often access patient data from remote locations using personal devices. ABAC enhances security by enforcing context-aware policies that restrict access based on device compliance, geographic location, and network security. For example, a policy might allow a telemedicine doctor to access a patient's medical history only if they are using a hospital-issued laptop with an encrypted connection. If the same doctor attempts to access records from a personal device on a public Wi-Fi network, ABAC can enforce additional authentication measures or deny access entirely.

Research data protection is another area where ABAC benefits the healthcare industry. Medical research institutions often handle large volumes of sensitive data, including genomic information, clinical trial results, and patient records. ABAC allows research facilities to define policies that protect this data while enabling secure collaboration between researchers. A policy could allow a university research team to access anonymized patient data for a clinical study but prevent access to personally identifiable information (PII) unless explicitly authorized by an ethics board. This ensures that medical research advances without violating patient privacy regulations.

ABAC also supports secure healthcare supply chain management by controlling access to pharmaceutical inventory, medical devices, and procurement systems. A hospital's ABAC policy might allow pharmacy staff to order medications but restrict order approvals to senior administrators with financial clearance. Similarly, a policy could ensure that only authorized technicians can access medical equipment configuration settings, preventing unauthorized modifications that could compromise patient safety.

Both government and healthcare sectors benefit from auditability and compliance automation provided by ABAC. Regulatory agencies require detailed logs of access control decisions, making it essential to track who accessed what data, when, and under what conditions. ABAC systems generate audit logs that provide transparency into access events, supporting forensic investigations, compliance reporting, and security audits. By integrating ABAC with identity governance tools, organizations can streamline access reviews, detect policy violations, and enforce corrective actions automatically.

The adoption of ABAC in government and healthcare continues to grow as organizations seek more adaptable and intelligent access control solutions. By leveraging real-time attributes, risk-based policies, and contextual awareness, ABAC enhances security while ensuring that authorized users can perform their roles efficiently. As cyber threats evolve and regulatory requirements become more stringent, ABAC will remain a vital component of secure and compliant access management in both sectors.

Auditing and Monitoring ABAC Policies

Auditing and monitoring Attribute-Based Access Control (ABAC) policies are essential for ensuring security, compliance, and operational efficiency. Unlike static access control models, ABAC dynamically evaluates attributes in real-time, which makes continuous monitoring necessary to detect policy violations, unauthorized access attempts, and anomalies. Organizations implementing ABAC must establish robust auditing mechanisms to track policy effectiveness, enforce compliance, and respond to security threats proactively.

One of the primary objectives of auditing ABAC policies is to ensure policy enforcement consistency. Since ABAC policies rely on attributes such as user identity, device security posture, time of access, and location, inconsistencies in attribute values or policy definitions can lead to unintended access grants or denials. Regular audits help organizations verify that policies are correctly implemented and that access control decisions align with business and security objectives. By reviewing historical access logs and policy evaluations, administrators can identify discrepancies and refine access rules accordingly.

Compliance auditing is another critical aspect of monitoring ABAC policies. Many regulatory frameworks, including GDPR, HIPAA, SOX, and PCI DSS, require organizations to enforce strict access controls and maintain audit trails of access events. ABAC's dynamic nature makes compliance enforcement more complex than traditional role-based access control models. Organizations must implement logging and reporting mechanisms that capture every access decision, attribute evaluation, and policy enforcement action. This allows auditors to review access patterns, validate policy adherence, and generate reports demonstrating compliance with regulatory requirements.

Access logs and event monitoring play a crucial role in auditing ABAC policies. Every access request in an ABAC system should generate a detailed log entry that includes:

The subject making the request (e.g., user, service, application).

The object being accessed (e.g., file, database, API endpoint).

The action performed (e.g., read, write, delete, execute).

The attributes evaluated (e.g., role, department, device compliance, network security level).

The final access decision (e.g., allow, deny, require additional authentication).

By aggregating this data into centralized Security Information and Event Management (SIEM) systems, organizations can analyze access trends, detect unauthorized activities, and generate compliance reports. Advanced analytics tools can also help correlate access logs with threat intelligence feeds, identifying suspicious access patterns that could indicate insider threats or compromised credentials.

Real-time policy monitoring and enforcement validation are necessary to ensure that ABAC policies function as intended. Organizations should deploy Policy Enforcement Points (PEPs) that intercept access requests and validate them against Policy Decision Points (PDPs) in real-time. If a policy misconfiguration or attribute inconsistency is detected, automated alerts should notify security teams for immediate investigation. Continuous policy validation helps organizations prevent privilege escalation attacks, unauthorized data exposure, and policy circumvention attempts.

One of the key challenges in ABAC auditing is tracking attribute changes over time. Since ABAC policies depend on dynamic attributes that change frequently—such as employee status, department assignments, or security risk scores—organizations must monitor how these changes affect access control decisions. For example, if an employee moves from the finance department to the IT department, their access privileges should be automatically updated to reflect their new responsibilities. Auditing attribute changes ensures that outdated or incorrect attribute values do not lead to security vulnerabilities or compliance violations.

Automated access reviews and policy audits help organizations streamline ABAC governance. Traditional access reviews in RBAC involve reviewing role assignments, but ABAC requires a more comprehensive approach that evaluates attribute usage and policy effectiveness. Organizations can automate access reviews by leveraging AI-driven identity governance solutions that analyze user access behavior, flag excessive permissions, and recommend policy adjustments. These automated audits reduce administrative overhead while ensuring continuous access control optimization.

Anomaly detection and behavioral analytics enhance ABAC policy monitoring by identifying deviations from normal access patterns. AI-driven security tools can analyze historical access data to establish a baseline of typical user behavior. If an access request deviates from this baseline—such as a user accessing a high-risk resource from an untrusted location—ABAC policies can trigger adaptive security responses, such as requiring additional authentication or temporarily restricting access. Behavioral analytics improve threat detection capabilities by identifying suspicious activities that traditional rule-based monitoring systems might overlook.

Forensic investigations and incident response benefit from detailed ABAC audit logs. In the event of a security breach or policy violation, security teams need access to detailed records that trace how an incident occurred. ABAC logs provide a clear trail of attribute evaluations, policy decisions, and user actions, enabling investigators to reconstruct attack sequences and identify vulnerabilities. Organizations should integrate ABAC auditing with forensic tools to facilitate post-incident analysis and improve future policy enforcement strategies.

Policy simulation and impact analysis provide additional value in auditing ABAC policies. Before deploying new policies or modifying existing ones, organizations can use simulation tools to test how policy changes will affect access control decisions. These simulations allow administrators to assess the impact of new policies on user access rights, identify potential conflicts, and refine policies before implementation. By proactively analyzing policy changes, organizations can prevent unintended access disruptions and security loopholes.

To further enhance ABAC auditing, organizations should implement real-time alerting and automated remediation mechanisms. When an access anomaly is detected—such as an unauthorized attempt to access sensitive data—automated security workflows can trigger immediate responses. For example, an ABAC system might automatically revoke access, initiate an identity verification process, or notify administrators for manual review. Automated remediation reduces response times and minimizes the risk of data breaches.

Another essential component of ABAC monitoring is policy lifecycle management. ABAC policies should not remain static; they must evolve with organizational changes, regulatory updates, and emerging security threats. Regular policy audits should assess whether existing policies still align with business objectives and compliance requirements. Organizations should establish a formal review process where security teams periodically evaluate policy effectiveness, update attribute definitions, and retire outdated policies that no longer serve a valid security purpose.

Organizations implementing ABAC at scale must also ensure cross-platform policy enforcement. In modern hybrid environments, where users access resources across on-premises systems, cloud applications, and mobile devices, ABAC policies must be consistently enforced across all platforms. Monitoring tools should provide visibility into access control events across distributed environments, ensuring that ABAC policies are applied uniformly regardless of access location.

Auditing and monitoring ABAC policies are critical for maintaining a secure, compliant, and efficient access control framework. By leveraging automated access reviews, real-time anomaly detection, forensic investigation tools, and policy lifecycle management, organizations can ensure that ABAC policies remain effective in protecting sensitive data and preventing unauthorized access. As ABAC adoption continues to grow, robust auditing and monitoring mechanisms will be essential for managing the complexity of dynamic access control and mitigating evolving security threats.

Combining RBAC and ABAC: The Best of Both Worlds

Role-Based Access Control (RBAC) and Attribute-Based Access Control (ABAC) are two widely used models for managing user permissions and enforcing security policies. While RBAC simplifies access management by assigning permissions based on predefined roles, ABAC provides greater flexibility by dynamically evaluating attributes to make real-time access decisions. Organizations often face challenges when choosing between RBAC and ABAC, as each model has its own advantages and limitations. Instead of treating them as mutually exclusive, many enterprises have begun integrating RBAC and ABAC to create a hybrid access control model that leverages the strengths of both approaches.

RBAC is one of the most commonly implemented access control models, particularly in large organizations with structured hierarchies. It simplifies access management by assigning users to roles, which in turn define their permissions. For example, an organization might define roles such as "HR Manager," "Finance Analyst," and "IT Administrator," each with predefined access rights. This approach reduces administrative overhead, as permissions do not need to be assigned individually to each user. However, RBAC has limitations in dynamic environments where access needs to be adjusted based on contextual factors such as location, device security, or real-time risk levels.

ABAC, on the other hand, allows access control decisions to be based on attributes rather than static role assignments. Attributes can include user properties (e.g., job title, department, security clearance), resource properties (e.g., data classification, ownership), action types (e.g., read, write, delete), and environmental factors (e.g., time of access, location, network security posture). ABAC policies evaluate multiple attributes in real-time to determine whether access should be granted or denied. This model provides greater granularity and flexibility compared to RBAC but can introduce complexity in policy management and attribute governance.

By combining RBAC and ABAC, organizations can achieve the best of both worlds—leveraging RBAC's simplicity for managing user roles while incorporating ABAC's dynamic, context-aware decision-making capabilities. A hybrid RBAC-ABAC model allows organizations to retain structured role assignments while refining access control decisions using attributes.

One common approach to integrating RBAC and ABAC is to use roles as attributes within an ABAC framework. Instead of defining rigid access permissions solely based on roles, organizations can treat roles as one of many attributes used in access decisions. For example, an ABAC policy might state:

"If user.role = 'Manager' AND user.department = 'Finance' AND access_time is between 08:00 and 18:00, THEN allow access to financial reports."

In this example, RBAC provides a baseline level of access control (the "Manager" role), while ABAC adds contextual conditions that refine the access decision. This approach ensures that access is granted based on both predefined roles and dynamic security requirements.

Another way to combine RBAC and ABAC is to use ABAC to supplement RBAC when additional granularity is needed. In many organizations, RBAC alone is sufficient for general access management, but certain high-risk or sensitive operations require more fine-grained control. For example, a hospital might implement RBAC to assign general access rights to doctors and nurses based on their roles, while ABAC is used to enforce additional conditions when accessing specific patient records.

A hybrid policy might include:

RBAC rule: "Doctors can access patient records in their assigned department."

ABAC refinement: "Doctors can access a patient's records only if they are assigned as the primary physician AND the access request is during working hours."

This ensures that while RBAC provides a general access framework, ABAC adds security measures based on real-time attributes, reducing the risk of unauthorized data access.

Hybrid RBAC-ABAC models also enhance privileged access management (PAM). In traditional RBAC, privileged users such as system administrators often have broad, persistent access to critical systems. By introducing ABAC, organizations can implement Just-In-Time (JIT) access, where privileged roles are only activated under specific conditions. For example, an IT administrator may only be granted system modification privileges if their request originates from a company-issued device within a secure network, reducing the risk of privilege misuse.

Compliance and regulatory adherence are also improved by integrating RBAC and ABAC. Many industries require strict access control policies to comply with regulations such as GDPR, HIPAA, and SOX. RBAC simplifies compliance reporting by clearly defining user roles and permissions, while ABAC ensures that access decisions align with real-time security and privacy requirements. For example, a financial institution might use RBAC to assign access rights to auditors but enforce ABAC policies to restrict access to customer data based on business justifications and time-based constraints.

Another advantage of combining RBAC and ABAC is simplified user onboarding and access provisioning. RBAC provides a structured approach to onboarding new employees by automatically assigning them roles based on their job function. However, ABAC can refine these assignments by considering additional attributes, such as employment status, probation periods, and security training completion. For example, a new employee in the IT department might be assigned the "IT Support" role through RBAC, but an ABAC policy may restrict their access to production systems until they complete mandatory cybersecurity training.

Despite its advantages, implementing a hybrid RBAC-ABAC model requires careful planning and governance. Organizations must:

Define clear role hierarchies to avoid unnecessary complexity.

Establish attribute governance to ensure that attribute data is accurate, reliable, and up to date.

Develop policy management tools that allow administrators to create and enforce RBAC-ABAC hybrid policies efficiently.

Continuously monitor access control decisions to detect anomalies and enforce compliance.

Organizations can use policy orchestration tools and identity governance solutions to manage hybrid access models effectively. These tools provide centralized management of roles, attributes, and policies, ensuring consistent enforcement across cloud, on-premises, and hybrid environments.

Combining RBAC and ABAC provides a scalable, flexible, and secure access control model that balances operational efficiency with dynamic security requirements. By leveraging RBAC's structured role management and ABAC's real-time decision-making capabilities, organizations can create an access control framework that meets modern security challenges while maintaining usability and compliance. The hybrid approach ensures that access policies remain adaptable to evolving business needs, making it a preferred choice for enterprises looking to enhance security without increasing administrative complexity.

Policy-Based Access Control (PBAC) vs. ABAC

Policy-Based Access Control (PBAC) and Attribute-Based Access Control (ABAC) are two advanced access control models designed to enforce security policies dynamically based on contextual factors. Both models move beyond traditional Role-Based Access Control (RBAC) by introducing fine-grained, rule-driven decision-making mechanisms. However, while they share similarities, PBAC and ABAC differ in their approach to defining and enforcing access control policies. Understanding these differences is crucial for organizations seeking to implement a flexible and scalable access control system that meets their security and compliance needs.

PBAC is a broad framework that governs access control based on predefined policies. It defines access rules using explicit policies that dictate when and how access is granted, based on a combination of user identity, resource attributes, and environmental conditions. PBAC is often used in enterprise environments where security policies must align with regulatory requirements, business rules, and risk management strategies. Policies in PBAC are centrally managed, providing a structured way to enforce compliance across an organization's IT infrastructure.

ABAC, on the other hand, is a specific implementation of policy-based access control that relies on attributes to make access decisions dynamically. In ABAC, access is granted or denied based on evaluating attributes related to the user (subject), the resource (object), the requested action, and the environmental context. Unlike RBAC, where access rights are statically assigned based on roles, ABAC allows for real-time decision-making based on multiple attribute conditions.

One of the key distinctions between PBAC and ABAC is their approach to policy enforcement. PBAC emphasizes high-level policy management, focusing on business rules and regulatory compliance. Organizations implementing PBAC often define broad policies such as:

"All financial transactions above $10,000 must require manager approval."

In contrast, ABAC focuses on fine-grained attribute evaluation, allowing policies to consider multiple contextual factors. An ABAC policy might state:

"If the user is a Finance Manager AND the transaction amount is below $10,000 AND the request originates from a corporate network, THEN allow approval."

This example illustrates how ABAC adds additional layers of conditional logic, making access control decisions more dynamic and context-aware.

Another major difference between PBAC and ABAC is policy complexity and scalability. PBAC is designed for large-scale policy enforcement where access control decisions must align with corporate governance requirements. Policies in PBAC tend to be rule-based and easier to interpret, making them well-suited for compliance-driven environments. In contrast, ABAC policies can become highly complex due to the large number of attributes involved. Managing a vast number of attribute-based conditions requires sophisticated attribute governance and automated policy management tools to prevent inconsistencies or policy sprawl.

PBAC is commonly used in regulatory and compliance-driven industries such as finance, healthcare, and government. Organizations in these sectors must enforce strict access controls based on legal and contractual obligations. PBAC simplifies compliance management by defining clear, structured policies that auditors can review and verify. For example, in a healthcare setting, a PBAC policy might state:

"Only licensed medical practitioners can approve prescription orders."

ABAC, however, extends this concept by incorporating dynamic conditions into access decisions. An ABAC policy for the same scenario might state:

"If the user is a licensed medical practitioner AND the prescription is for a registered patient AND the request is made during working hours, THEN allow approval."

This example highlights how ABAC adds additional layers of security by considering real-time contextual factors that PBAC alone may not cover.

A key advantage of ABAC over PBAC is real-time decision-making and risk-based access control. PBAC enforces predefined rules but does not inherently evaluate dynamic risk factors. ABAC, on the other hand, can integrate with risk engines and behavioral analytics to adjust access permissions based on detected threats. For example, an ABAC system can evaluate:

The user's security clearance level.

The device's compliance status (e.g., whether it has the latest security patches).

The geographic location of the access request.

The historical behavior of the user (e.g., unusual access patterns).

If an access request deviates from normal behavior, ABAC can dynamically enforce additional authentication steps or deny access outright. PBAC, being more static, lacks this level of adaptability unless explicitly integrated with real-time monitoring systems.

Implementation complexity is another area where PBAC and ABAC differ. PBAC is often easier to deploy because it relies on clearly defined policies that do not require extensive attribute management. Organizations implementing PBAC can define access rules in a centralized policy management system, making it simpler to administer. ABAC, by contrast, requires a robust attribute infrastructure, including accurate data sources, real-time synchronization, and ongoing attribute validation. Without proper attribute governance, ABAC policies can become difficult to manage and enforce consistently across distributed environments.

PBAC is typically integrated with policy orchestration platforms that allow administrators to create, modify, and enforce policies across an organization's IT ecosystem. These platforms provide visibility into policy compliance and facilitate audit reporting. ABAC, on the other hand, requires identity and access management (IAM) solutions that can evaluate attributes dynamically. Many organizations implement ABAC in combination with Security Information and Event Management (SIEM) systems to analyze real-time security events and adjust policies based on detected risks.

In multi-cloud and hybrid environments, organizations often combine PBAC and ABAC to achieve both compliance-driven policy enforcement and dynamic access control. PBAC provides a structured approach to defining overarching security policies, while ABAC refines these policies with contextual intelligence. For example, a PBAC policy might state:

"All remote access to corporate applications must require multi-factor authentication (MFA)."

An ABAC rule can further refine this policy:

"If the user is accessing from an unmanaged device OR from a high-risk country, THEN require additional identity verification before granting access."

This hybrid approach ensures that security policies remain both predictable and adaptable, providing organizations with a balance between compliance and security flexibility.

PBAC and ABAC each have their strengths, and choosing between them depends on an organization's security objectives, regulatory requirements, and IT environment. While PBAC is well-suited for organizations that need clear, structured policies for compliance, ABAC provides greater adaptability in dynamic, high-risk environments where contextual factors play a crucial role in access decisions. Many enterprises benefit from integrating both models, using PBAC for broad policy governance and ABAC for fine-grained, risk-aware access control. This combined approach ensures that organizations can meet both regulatory compliance standards and modern cybersecurity challenges effectively.

Risk-Based and Adaptive Access Control

Risk-based and adaptive access control are advanced security models that enable organizations to dynamically adjust access permissions based on real-time risk assessments and contextual factors. Traditional access control models, such as Role-Based Access Control (RBAC) and even Attribute-Based Access Control (ABAC), often rely on predefined policies that do not account for evolving security threats. Risk-based access control (RBAC, not to be confused with role-based access control) and adaptive access control introduce intelligence into access management by continuously evaluating risk factors and making access decisions that balance security and usability.

The foundation of risk-based access control lies in real-time risk assessments, which determine the likelihood of a security threat based on various factors. Instead of granting or denying access solely based on static roles or attributes, risk-based models calculate a risk score for each access request. This score is generated based on multiple inputs, such as user behavior, device health, network conditions, geolocation, and historical access patterns. If the calculated risk exceeds a predefined threshold, additional security measures may be enforced, such as multi-factor authentication (MFA), temporary access restrictions, or even an outright denial of access.

For example, a finance employee attempting to access a company's payment processing system from a corporate office on a company-issued laptop might be assigned a low-risk score, allowing seamless access. However, if the same employee tries to access the system from an unrecognized device in a foreign country, the system may classify this request as high-risk, triggering an additional identity verification step before access is granted.

Behavioral analytics and anomaly detection play a crucial role in risk-based access control. By analyzing historical access patterns and user behavior, organizations can establish a baseline of normal activity. When deviations from this baseline occur—such as a sudden spike in login attempts, access requests outside usual working hours, or multiple failed authentication attempts—the system can dynamically adjust access permissions based on the perceived risk. This adaptive approach prevents unauthorized access while minimizing disruptions for legitimate users.

Adaptive access control expands on risk-based access control by continuously adjusting security policies in real-time based on evolving threats and environmental conditions. Unlike static access control models that grant permissions indefinitely until manually revoked, adaptive access control monitors user activity and dynamically modifies access levels as risks change.

One of the most effective implementations of adaptive access control is step-up authentication, where users are granted initial access with minimal friction, but additional authentication is required when risk levels increase. For example, an employee may be allowed to view sensitive customer data with a single sign-on (SSO) login under normal conditions. However, if the employee attempts to download large volumes of customer data, the system may prompt for an additional authentication factor, such as a biometric scan or a one-time passcode. This prevents data exfiltration without disrupting routine business operations.

Risk-based and adaptive access control are particularly valuable in zero-trust security architectures, where access is never assumed based on prior authentication. In a zero-trust model, every access request is verified based on current risk levels, ensuring that users, devices, and applications must continuously prove their trustworthiness before gaining access. Adaptive access control aligns with zero-trust principles by enforcing continuous verification, rather than relying on static authentication events.

Device posture assessment is another critical component of risk-based and adaptive access control. Organizations must ensure that users access corporate resources only from secure, compliant devices. If a device is found to be missing security patches, running outdated software, or connected to an untrusted network, the system can dynamically restrict access or require additional security verification before allowing entry. This approach prevents malware-infected or compromised devices from accessing sensitive systems.

In cloud and hybrid environments, risk-based and adaptive access control provide an added layer of security by ensuring that access policies are applied consistently across multiple platforms. Organizations that operate in multi-cloud environments can enforce risk-based policies that prevent unauthorized access to cloud applications based on geographic location, IP reputation, or suspicious login behavior. For example, a policy may block access to cloud storage services if the access request comes from a country where the organization does not conduct business.

Risk-based and adaptive access control also enhance privileged access management (PAM) by ensuring that users with elevated permissions do not retain unnecessary privileges indefinitely. Instead of granting privileged users permanent access to critical systems, organizations can implement just-in-time (JIT) access, where administrative privileges are granted only when needed and revoked once the task is completed. This minimizes the risk of insider threats and unauthorized privilege escalation.

Integration with artificial intelligence (AI) and machine learning (ML) further enhances risk-based and adaptive access control. AI-driven security systems can analyze large volumes of access logs, detect patterns indicative of security threats, and automatically adjust policies in response. For example, an AI system might detect that a user's login credentials have appeared in a dark web data breach and proactively force a password reset or block the user's access until identity verification is completed.

Organizations implementing risk-based and adaptive access control must also ensure compliance with regulatory requirements. Many industry regulations, such as the General Data Protection Regulation (GDPR), the Health Insurance Portability and Accountability Act (HIPAA), and the Payment Card Industry Data Security Standard (PCI DSS), mandate strict access controls and data protection measures. Risk-based models align with these regulations by dynamically enforcing security controls based on data sensitivity, user roles, and real-time risk levels.

Despite its advantages, risk-based and adaptive access control come with challenges, particularly in policy management and user experience. Organizations must carefully design access policies to balance security with usability. If adaptive policies are too strict, they can create unnecessary friction for legitimate users, leading to frustration and decreased productivity. Conversely, if policies are too lenient, security risks may go undetected. Organizations should regularly review and fine-tune risk thresholds to ensure that security measures align with actual threat levels.

Another challenge is attribute and data quality management. Since risk-based access control relies on real-time data inputs, organizations must ensure that risk assessment models receive accurate, timely, and relevant data. Poorly maintained attributes, inconsistent user profiles, or unreliable device telemetry can lead to incorrect access decisions. Implementing automated attribute synchronization and real-time monitoring helps maintain data integrity and ensures that access control decisions remain accurate.

Risk-based and adaptive access control are rapidly becoming the standard approach to access management in modern IT environments. By leveraging real-time risk assessments, behavioral analytics, AI-driven security insights, and contextual intelligence, organizations can implement dynamic access control models that improve security without compromising user experience. These models provide the flexibility needed to adapt to evolving cyber threats while ensuring compliance with industry regulations and corporate security policies. As cybersecurity challenges continue to grow, risk-based and adaptive access control will play an increasingly vital role in protecting sensitive data, preventing unauthorized access, and enabling secure digital transformation.

Zero Trust and the Role of RBAC/ABAC

Zero Trust is a modern security framework that eliminates the traditional assumption of trust within an organization's network. Instead of granting broad access based on network location, Zero Trust enforces strict identity verification and continuous access control based on the principle of "never trust, always verify." This model ensures that every access request is authenticated, authorized, and evaluated against security policies before being granted. Role-Based Access Control (RBAC) and Attribute-Based Access Control (ABAC) ·play crucial roles in implementing Zero Trust, as they provide structured mechanisms for managing access based on predefined roles and real-time attributes.

RBAC has been widely used in enterprise environments to manage user permissions by assigning access rights based on predefined roles. A user is granted permissions according to their job function, department, or business needs, simplifying access management while reducing administrative overhead. However, RBAC alone is not sufficient for a Zero Trust architecture because it does not dynamically evaluate access requests based on risk levels, contextual factors, or real-time threats. Once a user is assigned a role, they typically retain those permissions indefinitely unless manually updated by administrators.

ABAC, on the other hand, aligns more closely with Zero Trust principles by enforcing context-aware access control. Unlike RBAC, which assigns access based on static roles, ABAC dynamically evaluates attributes such as user identity, device security posture, geographic location, time of access, and behavioral analytics. This approach ensures that access decisions are continuously verified based on current risk conditions. For example, even if an employee has a role that permits access to a sensitive database, an ABAC policy could deny access if the request originates from an untrusted network or an unmanaged device.

A hybrid RBAC-ABAC approach is often the best strategy for implementing Zero Trust in large enterprises. While RBAC provides a structured foundation for managing role assignments, ABAC introduces granular access control policies that adjust permissions dynamically. This hybrid model enables organizations to enforce strict access controls while maintaining flexibility to adapt to changing security conditions.

One of the key Zero Trust principles is least privilege access, which ensures that users and systems only have the minimum access necessary to perform their tasks. RBAC alone can enforce least privilege by restricting users to predefined roles, but it lacks adaptability when users require temporary or conditional access. ABAC enhances least privilege enforcement by evaluating real-time conditions before granting access. For instance, a security administrator might have full system privileges when working from a corporate-managed laptop but have restricted access when logging in from a personal device.

Another critical aspect of Zero Trust is continuous authentication and adaptive access control. Traditional authentication mechanisms, such as username and password verification, are no longer sufficient in Zero Trust environments. Instead, organizations must implement risk-based access control that continuously evaluates user activity and requires additional authentication when anomalies are detected. ABAC plays a key role in this process by enforcing step-up authentication when risk levels increase. For example, a user accessing a financial application from an unusual location might be required to complete multi-factor authentication (MFA) before proceeding.

RBAC and ABAC also contribute to identity verification and device trust, two essential components of Zero Trust. Organizations implementing Zero Trust must validate not only the user's identity but also the security posture of the device being used for access. ABAC enables organizations to define policies that restrict access based on device attributes such as operating system version, patch level, or endpoint security compliance. If a device does not meet security standards, access can be denied or restricted until remediation actions are taken.

Micro-segmentation, another key principle of Zero Trust, is strengthened through RBAC and ABAC. Micro-segmentation involves dividing the network into smaller, isolated segments to limit lateral movement in the event of a security breach. RBAC can help enforce micro-segmentation by defining role-based access controls for specific network segments, while ABAC refines access control by incorporating real-time security intelligence. For example, if an attacker compromises a user account, ABAC policies can detect abnormal behavior and restrict the user's access to critical systems, preventing further compromise.

Privileged Access Management (PAM) is another area where RBAC and ABAC support Zero Trust implementation. Privileged users, such as system administrators, often have elevated access to critical infrastructure. In traditional models, privileged accounts are statically assigned and can be exploited by attackers if credentials are compromised. By integrating RBAC with ABAC, organizations can enforce just-in-time (JIT) access, where privileged users receive temporary, role-based access only when needed and only under specific conditions. If an administrator requests elevated privileges outside of normal working hours or from an unknown device, ABAC policies can require additional verification before granting access.

Cloud security and Zero Trust also benefit from the integration of RBAC and ABAC. As organizations migrate workloads to cloud environments, enforcing consistent access control policies across multiple cloud providers becomes a challenge. RBAC provides a structured way to define access rights within cloud services, but ABAC ensures cross-cloud policy enforcement by evaluating dynamic attributes before granting access. A Zero Trust cloud security model might include policies such as:

RBAC rule: "Cloud engineers can manage cloud infrastructure based on assigned roles."

ABAC policy refinement: "Cloud engineers can modify infrastructure only when using a managed device, from an approved geographic location, and with an active VPN connection."

This approach ensures that cloud access policies remain both structured and dynamic, reducing the risk of unauthorized access and compliance violations.

Regulatory compliance and auditability are strengthened when RBAC and ABAC are used together in Zero Trust implementations. Many industry regulations, such as GDPR, HIPAA, and NIST 800-207 (Zero Trust Architecture), require organizations to enforce strict access controls and maintain detailed audit logs. RBAC simplifies compliance reporting by defining clear role-based permissions, while ABAC provides detailed logging of attribute-based access decisions. This combination ensures that access control policies remain transparent, enforceable, and aligned with regulatory requirements.

Organizations implementing Zero Trust with RBAC and ABAC must focus on policy management, automation, and continuous monitoring. Automated policy orchestration tools help security teams define and enforce RBAC-ABAC hybrid policies across on-premises, cloud, and hybrid environments. Security Information and Event Management (SIEM) systems integrate with access control frameworks to monitor access attempts, detect anomalies, and respond to security incidents in real time.

Zero Trust requires a paradigm shift in access management, moving away from static permissions toward continuous verification and adaptive security policies. RBAC provides the foundation for structured access control, while ABAC enhances flexibility and real-time decision-making. By integrating both models, organizations can implement a robust Zero Trust framework that enforces least privilege, adapts to evolving threats, and ensures compliance with industry standards. As cybersecurity risks continue to evolve, the combination of RBAC and ABAC will remain a critical component of modern Zero Trust architectures, helping organizations achieve a secure, scalable, and resilient access control strategy.

Next-Generation Access Control Models

As digital transformation accelerates, traditional access control models such as Role-Based Access Control (RBAC) and Attribute-Based Access Control (ABAC) are evolving to meet the demands of modern cybersecurity threats, regulatory compliance, and dynamic IT environments. Next-generation access control models integrate emerging technologies, risk-based decision-making, and automation to provide more adaptive, intelligent, and scalable access control solutions. These models aim to enhance security, improve operational efficiency, and ensure seamless user experiences without compromising protection.

One of the most prominent next-generation models is Risk-Adaptive Access Control (RAdAC), which builds on ABAC by incorporating real-time risk assessments into access control decisions. Unlike traditional models that rely on predefined policies, RAdAC continuously evaluates contextual factors such as user behavior, threat intelligence, and environmental conditions to adjust access permissions dynamically. This approach enables organizations to grant, deny, or restrict access based on the perceived risk level of a request. For example, if a user attempts to access sensitive financial data from an unfamiliar device, RAdAC can require additional authentication, limit access to read-only mode, or delay access until security verification is completed.

Another emerging model is Continuous Adaptive Trust (CAT), which aligns with the Zero Trust security framework. CAT moves beyond traditional authentication methods by enforcing continuous authentication and authorization throughout a user's session. Instead of relying on a single login event, CAT evaluates real-time attributes such as device security posture, application usage patterns, and network anomalies to determine whether a session should remain active. If a user's behavior deviates from normal activity—such as accessing restricted files unexpectedly or attempting to log in from multiple locations simultaneously—CAT can revoke access or escalate security measures without requiring manual intervention.

Policy-Based Access Control (PBAC) is another next-generation approach that extends ABAC by introducing centralized policy management and automation. PBAC allows organizations to define high-level security policies that dynamically translate into granular access controls based on contextual attributes. This model is particularly useful in regulatory environments where organizations must enforce strict data access rules based on compliance requirements. Instead of manually managing user permissions, PBAC automates policy enforcement across multiple applications, cloud environments, and hybrid infrastructures. For example, a PBAC system in a healthcare organization can automatically enforce HIPAA-compliant access rules based on user roles, patient consent status, and legal jurisdiction.

Context-Aware Access Control (CAAC) introduces real-time situational awareness into access control policies. CAAC enhances traditional models by considering environmental factors such as geolocation, device security state, biometric authentication, and AI-driven threat detection. This model is widely adopted in cloud security, where users access corporate applications from diverse locations and devices. A CAAC implementation may allow an employee to access company resources freely from a corporate office but restrict access when logging in from an untrusted public Wi-Fi network. By continuously monitoring access requests in real time, CAAC reduces the risk of credential misuse, unauthorized access, and insider threats.

Just-In-Time (JIT) Access Control is gaining popularity in privileged access management (PAM) and cloud security. Unlike static role-based access models where users retain permanent access to critical systems, JIT access grants temporary permissions only when needed. This reduces the risk of over-privileged accounts and minimizes the attack surface for insider threats and credential-based attacks. For example, a cloud engineer may need elevated permissions to modify a server configuration, but instead of being permanently assigned admin rights, JIT access ensures that the privilege is granted only for the duration of the task and is revoked immediately afterward.

Artificial Intelligence (AI) and Machine Learning (ML) are playing a transformative role in AI-Driven Access Control, where access decisions are influenced by behavioral analytics and predictive modeling. AI-driven models analyze historical access patterns, detect anomalies, and recommend or enforce policy changes based on observed trends. For instance, an AI-powered access control system can recognize that a software developer only accesses certain repositories during normal business hours. If an access request occurs outside expected parameters—such as an unusual time, location, or request volume—the system can trigger additional authentication or deny access automatically.

Federated Access Control is becoming increasingly important as organizations expand their use of multi-cloud environments, SaaS applications, and third-party integrations. Traditional access control models struggle with managing access across distributed systems and partner networks. Federated access allows multiple organizations or business units to share identity and access management (IAM) frameworks securely while enforcing consistent access policies. For example, a global enterprise operating across multiple cloud providers can implement federated access to ensure that employees can authenticate seamlessly across AWS, Microsoft Azure, and Google Cloud while maintaining centralized policy enforcement.

Decentralized Identity and Blockchain-Based Access Control represent a cutting-edge approach to identity verification and access management. Unlike traditional IAM systems that rely on centralized identity providers, decentralized identity models allow users to own and control their digital identities using blockchain technology. This reduces reliance on third-party authentication services and mitigates risks associated with single points of failure. Blockchain-based access control ensures that access records are immutable, transparent, and verifiable, making it an ideal solution for securing sensitive transactions in industries such as finance, healthcare, and government.

Quantum-Resistant Access Control is an emerging field that anticipates the impact of quantum computing on cybersecurity. As quantum computers become more powerful, traditional encryption methods may become obsolete, potentially exposing existing access control systems to attacks. Next-generation access models are exploring quantum-resistant cryptographic techniques to future-proof authentication and authorization mechanisms. Organizations investing in quantum-safe security strategies aim to implement cryptographic agility, ensuring that access control policies remain secure even in the face of quantum computing advancements.

Organizations adopting next-generation access control models must focus on automation, orchestration, and interoperability to ensure seamless enforcement across on-premises, cloud, and hybrid environments. Security teams must also integrate these models with Security Information and Event Management (SIEM) systems, Endpoint Detection and Response (EDR) solutions, and Identity Governance tools to maintain continuous visibility and threat detection.

As cybersecurity threats continue to evolve, next-generation access control models provide the intelligence, adaptability, and resilience required to protect sensitive systems and data. By leveraging AI-driven analytics, risk-adaptive decision-making, decentralized identity frameworks, and real-time contextual awareness, organizations can create access control strategies that dynamically adjust to emerging security challenges while maintaining operational efficiency and compliance. The future of access control lies in automation, intelligence, and continuous security validation, ensuring that organizations can respond to cyber threats proactively while enabling secure and seamless user experiences.

Identity and Access Management (IAM) Integration with RBAC/ABAC

Identity and Access Management (IAM) is a foundational component of enterprise security, ensuring that the right individuals have appropriate access to systems, applications, and data. As organizations expand their IT environments across on-premises, cloud, and hybrid infrastructures, integrating IAM with Role-Based Access Control (RBAC) and Attribute-Based Access Control (ABAC) has become essential. By combining IAM with RBAC and ABAC, organizations can enforce structured, scalable, and dynamic access policies that balance security, compliance, and usability.

IAM provides a centralized framework for managing identities, authentication, and authorization across an organization's digital ecosystem. It includes identity lifecycle management, authentication services, access provisioning, and policy enforcement. IAM solutions integrate with RBAC and ABAC to streamline access control, automate policy enforcement, and provide real-time visibility into access decisions.

RBAC has been widely adopted in IAM systems due to its simplicity and ease of administration. It assigns permissions based on predefined roles, reducing the complexity of managing individual user permissions. For example, an IAM system may define roles such as "HR Manager," "Finance Analyst," and "IT Administrator," each with specific access rights to applications and resources. When a new employee joins the organization, IAM can automatically assign them a role based on their department and job function, simplifying the onboarding process. However, RBAC alone has limitations in dynamic and risk-based access control scenarios, where access decisions need to adapt to contextual factors.

ABAC enhances IAM by incorporating real-time attributes into access control decisions. Unlike RBAC, which relies solely on role assignments, ABAC evaluates attributes such as user identity, device security posture, location, time of access, and behavioral risk levels. Integrating IAM with ABAC enables fine-grained access control that adapts to changing security conditions. For example, an IAM-integrated ABAC system can enforce policies such as:

A sales representative can access customer data only if they are in their assigned region and using a company-managed device.

A software engineer can modify production code only if they are working within business hours and have received approval from a manager.

A financial analyst can access sensitive reports only if their risk score is below a predefined threshold.

IAM platforms provide the attribute repositories and policy enforcement mechanisms needed to implement ABAC effectively. They integrate with directory services (e.g., Active Directory, LDAP), security monitoring tools, and cloud identity providers to fetch real-time attributes and enforce access policies dynamically.

A critical aspect of IAM integration with RBAC and ABAC is identity lifecycle management, which governs the creation, modification, and deactivation of user accounts. IAM automates user provisioning and deprovisioning based on role assignments and attribute changes. When an employee joins an organization, IAM assigns them an appropriate role (RBAC) and attributes (ABAC), ensuring they receive the necessary permissions. If their job role changes, IAM updates their access rights dynamically, preventing privilege accumulation and reducing insider threats. When an employee leaves, IAM automatically revokes access, ensuring that former employees do not retain unauthorized access to corporate resources.

Single Sign-On (SSO) and Multi-Factor Authentication (MFA) play crucial roles in IAM integration with RBAC and ABAC. SSO simplifies authentication by allowing users to access multiple applications with a single set of credentials. IAM integrates SSO with RBAC to provide role-based authentication workflows, ensuring that users are authenticated based on their assigned roles. ABAC enhances SSO security by enforcing adaptive authentication policies, where authentication requirements adjust based on contextual factors. For example, an IAM-integrated ABAC system might require MFA if a user logs in from an unfamiliar device or a high-risk location, reducing the likelihood of credential compromise.

IAM integration with RBAC and ABAC also improves cloud security and hybrid access management. Organizations operating in multi-cloud environments must enforce consistent access policies across AWS, Microsoft Azure, Google Cloud, and SaaS applications. IAM acts as a centralized access management layer, ensuring that RBAC and ABAC policies are applied uniformly across cloud platforms. This prevents policy fragmentation, where access rules differ between cloud services, creating security gaps.

Privileged Access Management (PAM) benefits from IAM integration with RBAC and ABAC by enforcing just-in-time (JIT) access controls. Privileged accounts, such as system administrators and security engineers, require elevated permissions to perform critical tasks. Instead of granting permanent privileged access, IAM-integrated ABAC policies can dynamically assign temporary, least-privilege access based on job function, security clearance, and risk assessment. If an administrator attempts to modify firewall configurations from an untrusted network, IAM can block access or require additional approvals, reducing the risk of misconfigurations and insider threats.

IAM also supports auditability and compliance by providing detailed access logs, policy enforcement reports, and real-time monitoring. Regulatory frameworks such as GDPR, HIPAA, and NIST 800-53 require organizations to maintain strict access controls and audit trails. IAM systems integrated with RBAC and ABAC generate comprehensive access logs that capture:

Who accessed which resources

When access occurred

The attributes used in the access decision

Whether access was granted or denied

Security teams use these logs for forensic investigations, compliance reporting, and real-time anomaly detection. IAM platforms can also integrate with Security Information and Event Management (SIEM) systems to correlate access control events with security alerts, improving threat detection and incident response.

Automated access reviews and recertifications are another key advantage of IAM integration with RBAC and ABAC. Traditional access reviews are often manual and time-consuming, leading to delays in detecting excessive or outdated permissions. IAM automates access reviews by leveraging RBAC role assignments and ABAC attribute evaluations. If an employee's job role changes, IAM can trigger an automatic review, ensuring that their access rights remain aligned with business needs and compliance requirements.

IAM integration with Zero Trust security models further strengthens identity-based access control. Zero Trust operates under the principle of continuous verification and least privilege, requiring every access request to be authenticated and authorized dynamically. IAM-enforced RBAC establishes baseline access permissions, while ABAC refines access control based on real-time security conditions. This ensures that access decisions are continuously evaluated, preventing implicit trust and reducing lateral movement risks in enterprise networks.

Organizations implementing IAM with RBAC and ABAC must focus on scalability, automation, and governance. IAM policies should be:

Centrally managed to ensure consistency across on-premises, cloud, and hybrid environments.

Continuously monitored to detect and respond to unauthorized access attempts.

Automatically updated to reflect changes in user roles, security attributes, and risk levels.

IAM integration with RBAC and ABAC is essential for modern cybersecurity strategies, enabling organizations to enforce structured, dynamic, and intelligent access control. By leveraging role-based assignments for simplicity and attribute-based policies for flexibility, organizations can create a secure, scalable, and adaptive IAM framework that protects sensitive data, enhances compliance, and improves user experience. As cyber threats evolve, IAM-integrated RBAC and ABAC will remain critical for managing identity security in complex IT ecosystems.

Access Control in Multi-Tenant and Cloud Environments

Access control in multi-tenant and cloud environments presents unique challenges due to the shared infrastructure, distributed nature, and dynamic resource allocation of cloud computing. Organizations must implement robust security policies to ensure that data and resources remain protected while enabling seamless access for authorized users. Traditional access control models such as Role-Based Access Control (RBAC) and Attribute-Based Access Control (ABAC) must be adapted to address cloud-specific security risks, compliance requirements, and multi-tenant considerations.

In a multi-tenant environment, multiple organizations, business units, or customers share the same cloud infrastructure while maintaining strict separation of data and resources. Cloud service providers (CSPs) implement logical isolation mechanisms to prevent unauthorized access between tenants, but organizations are responsible for defining and enforcing access control policies within their tenant space. RBAC and ABAC are commonly used to manage permissions across users, applications, and services within multi-tenant cloud platforms.

RBAC provides a structured way to assign permissions based on predefined roles. In a multi-tenant cloud environment, RBAC can be used to define roles such as Tenant Administrator, Developer, Security Analyst, and Support Engineer, each with different levels of access to cloud resources. For example, a Tenant Administrator may have full control over the cloud environment, while a Support Engineer can only access diagnostic tools but cannot modify configurations. However,

RBAC alone is insufficient in highly dynamic cloud environments, where access needs to be adjusted based on real-time security conditions and contextual factors.

ABAC enhances access control in multi-tenant and cloud environments by incorporating dynamic attributes into access decisions. Unlike RBAC, which assigns permissions based on static roles, ABAC evaluates user identity, device security posture, geographic location, time of access, and network conditions before granting access. This ensures that access control policies adapt to contextual risks and compliance requirements. For example, an ABAC policy may allow a user to manage cloud storage services only if they are connecting from a corporate network and using an encrypted device. If the user attempts access from an unknown location, the system can enforce additional authentication measures or restrict access entirely.

One of the major security challenges in multi-cloud environments is ensuring consistent access policies across multiple cloud providers such as AWS, Microsoft Azure, and Google Cloud Platform. Each cloud provider has its own IAM framework, making it difficult to enforce a unified access control strategy. Organizations must implement federated identity and centralized access management to ensure that users can authenticate seamlessly across cloud platforms while maintaining consistent security policies.

Federated identity allows organizations to extend their existing on-premises IAM systems to cloud environments. By integrating with Security Assertion Markup Language (SAML), OpenID Connect (OIDC), and OAuth 2.0, organizations can enable Single Sign-On (SSO) across multiple cloud applications. This reduces password fatigue, simplifies authentication, and ensures that access control policies remain centrally managed.

Just-In-Time (JIT) access control is another critical mechanism in cloud security. Instead of granting users persistent permissions, JIT access ensures that privileges are assigned only when needed and for a limited duration. For example, a cloud engineer requiring temporary administrative access to troubleshoot a server issue may be granted elevated privileges for a specific task, with permissions automatically revoked once the task is completed. JIT access minimizes privilege abuse risks and enhances least privilege enforcement.

Access control policies in Software-as-a-Service (SaaS) environments must also address tenant data segregation to prevent unauthorized cross-tenant access. Cloud providers implement logical isolation techniques such as attribute-based tenancy tagging to ensure that each tenant's data remains separate. For example, an ABAC policy may enforce:

A sales representative can only view customer records assigned to their tenant ID.

A marketing team member can access shared reports but cannot modify data belonging to another tenant.

By enforcing tenant-aware access control policies, organizations can protect sensitive data and prevent accidental data exposure between tenants.

Cloud network security and access control must also be integrated into access policies. Organizations should enforce network segmentation and Zero Trust principles to restrict access based on network location, VPN usage, and endpoint security status. An example ABAC policy may state:

Cloud administrators can modify virtual machines only if they are connected via a company-approved VPN.

Database access is denied if the request originates from an untrusted public IP address.

Zero Trust security models complement RBAC and ABAC by ensuring that every access request is continuously verified based on risk assessments. Instead of granting implicit trust after authentication, Zero Trust ensures that access is dynamically adjusted based on real-time security conditions.

Compliance and regulatory considerations are critical in multi-tenant cloud environments, where organizations must comply with industry standards such as GDPR, HIPAA, and ISO 27001. Cloud access control policies should enforce data residency, encryption, and audit logging to meet regulatory requirements. For example, a financial institution operating in multiple regions may need to enforce ABAC policies ensuring that:

Customer financial data is accessible only to employees within the same geographic region.

Audit logs are retained for a predefined period to meet regulatory mandates.

IAM solutions integrated with RBAC and ABAC help organizations maintain auditability, traceability, and policy enforcement across multi-cloud environments. Cloud providers offer Cloud Access Security Brokers (CASBs) to monitor access control events, detect anomalies, and enforce compliance policies.

Organizations must also address cross-cloud identity governance, ensuring that user provisioning, deprovisioning, and policy enforcement remain consistent across different cloud platforms. Automated IAM workflows help manage access reviews, certification processes, and compliance reporting, reducing administrative overhead while maintaining security alignment across hybrid cloud environments.

Cloud-based access control models continue to evolve with AI-driven security analytics and machine learning. By integrating AI with IAM, organizations can:

Detect abnormal access patterns and enforce adaptive security policies.

Automate policy recommendations based on user behavior.

Reduce manual access review efforts with AI-driven identity governance.

The complexity of access control in multi-tenant and cloud environments requires organizations to adopt a layered security approach that combines RBAC for structured role assignments, ABAC for contextual enforcement, and Zero Trust for continuous verification. By integrating these models with IAM solutions, organizations can secure cloud workloads, protect sensitive data, and enforce compliance policies while enabling seamless access management.

Implementing Just-In-Time Access Control

Just-In-Time (JIT) Access Control is an advanced security model designed to enforce the principle of least privilege by granting access only when needed and for a limited duration. Unlike traditional access control models, where users are assigned permanent permissions based on roles or attributes, JIT access ensures that privileges are dynamically granted based on real-time requests, security conditions, and predefined approval workflows. This approach significantly reduces the attack surface, minimizes privilege misuse, and enhances security in dynamic IT environments, including cloud infrastructures, DevOps pipelines, and privileged access management (PAM).

One of the key motivations for implementing JIT access control is reducing standing privileges. In traditional access control models, users—especially privileged administrators—are assigned broad, persistent permissions to systems, databases, and applications. If a hacker compromises an account with high-standing privileges, they can move laterally within the network, escalate their access, and cause significant damage. JIT access control mitigates this risk by ensuring that elevated privileges are temporary, time-bound, and granted only when necessary.

A common implementation of JIT access control is through on-demand privilege elevation, where users request access only when needed. For example, an IT administrator who needs to modify firewall rules or restart cloud instances can request temporary administrative privileges rather than holding permanent access. Once the task is completed, the privileges are automatically revoked, preventing unnecessary exposure.

JIT access control can be implemented in various ways, depending on the security requirements and technology stack of an organization.

Time-Based JIT Access

Time-based JIT access grants permissions for a predefined time window before automatically expiring. This model is useful for scenarios where temporary access is required for maintenance, troubleshooting, or project-based work. For example:

A database administrator can request write access to a production database for 60 minutes to resolve an incident.

A software developer can be granted deployment permissions for 24 hours when rolling out a new application update.

A contractor working on a short-term project receives access to specific resources for the duration of their contract, with automatic expiration at the contract's end date.

This model ensures that no unnecessary access persists beyond the required timeframe, reducing security risks associated with abandoned or orphaned privileges.

Approval-Based JIT Access

Approval-based JIT access requires explicit authorization before access is granted. This model is often used for high-risk privileges, where access requests must be reviewed and approved by security teams, managers, or system owners. For example:

A cloud engineer requesting administrative access to a Kubernetes cluster must receive approval from a security officer or DevOps lead before the access is granted.

A finance analyst requesting access to a sensitive financial report must obtain manager approval to ensure compliance with corporate governance policies.

A privileged account request for a system modification requires a multi-level approval chain, ensuring that multiple stakeholders verify the necessity of the request.

This approach adds an extra layer of security, ensuring that access is granted based on business justification and not merely based on preassigned roles.

Zero Standing Privileges (ZSP) with JIT Access

JIT access control is a fundamental component of Zero Standing Privileges (ZSP), an approach that ensures that no user has permanent elevated access by default. In a ZSP model:

All users start with minimal access.

Access is requested and granted dynamically, based on real-time security checks.

Access is automatically revoked once the task is completed.

This approach is especially effective in cloud security and DevOps environments, where developers, administrators, and security teams need temporary permissions to deploy code, manage infrastructure, or investigate security incidents.

Risk-Based JIT Access

Risk-based JIT access integrates with real-time security analytics and threat intelligence to adjust access policies dynamically. Instead of granting access solely based on role or attribute-based conditions, risk-based JIT access evaluates factors such as:

Device security posture (e.g., is the user accessing from a company-managed device with up-to-date security patches?).

Location (e.g., is the request coming from a high-risk country or an unfamiliar IP address?).

Behavioral analytics (e.g., is this access request consistent with the user's normal activity?).

If the system detects anomalies or elevated risks, it may enforce additional authentication steps, require additional approvals, or deny access altogether. For example, if a system administrator suddenly requests access to a restricted database from an untrusted location, the system could flag the request as suspicious and require biometric authentication or managerial approval before proceeding.

JIT Access in Cloud and DevOps Security

Cloud environments, DevOps workflows, and containerized applications require flexible access control that does not rely on static permissions. JIT access ensures that developers, engineers, and security teams receive only the permissions they need, when they need them, and for as long as required.

For example:

A DevOps engineer working with AWS IAM, Azure RBAC, or Google Cloud IAM can request temporary access to cloud resources instead of holding permanent admin privileges.

A developer deploying new code to a Kubernetes cluster can be granted temporary access to deployment pipelines, which expires automatically after the deployment is complete.

A security auditor investigating a security event can request read-only access to logs and monitoring tools for the duration of the investigation.

JIT access in cloud environments significantly reduces attack surfaces, privilege abuse, and misconfigurations by ensuring that access is time-limited and need-based.

Automating JIT Access with IAM and Security Tools

Organizations implementing JIT access control can integrate it with Identity and Access Management (IAM) solutions, Privileged Access Management (PAM) tools, and Security Orchestration platforms. Solutions such as:

Azure AD Privileged Identity Management (PIM) for managing JIT access to cloud resources.

Google Cloud IAM and AWS Identity Center for enabling JIT access to cloud workloads.

CyberArk, BeyondTrust, and HashiCorp Vault for JIT privilege escalation and secret management.

These tools automate access provisioning, approval workflows, and access expiration, ensuring that JIT policies are enforced consistently.

Challenges and Best Practices for Implementing JIT Access

While JIT access control enhances security, organizations must address potential challenges such as user friction, policy enforcement complexity, and integration with existing IAM frameworks.

Best practices for JIT access implementation include:

Defining clear access policies that specify when, how, and for how long JIT access is granted.

Automating access requests and approvals to reduce manual overhead.

Integrating with behavioral analytics and risk-based security tools to enforce adaptive JIT policies.

Ensuring auditability and compliance by maintaining detailed access logs, approvals, and revocation events.

By adopting a JIT access control model, organizations reduce security risks, enforce least privilege access, and improve governance, making it an essential strategy for modern cybersecurity and cloud security architectures.

User Behavior Analytics and Access Control Decisions

User Behavior Analytics (UBA) is an advanced security approach that leverages machine learning, artificial intelligence, and data analytics to monitor, analyze, and detect unusual user activities. In modern access control systems, integrating UBA enhances security by identifying anomalous behavior patterns and dynamically adjusting access control decisions in real time. Traditional access control models, such as Role-Based Access Control (RBAC) and Attribute-Based Access Control (ABAC), rely on predefined rules and policies to grant or deny access. However, these models often fail to detect insider threats, compromised credentials, and privilege abuse because they do not continuously evaluate user behavior. UBA bridges this gap by identifying deviations from normal access patterns, detecting risky activities, and triggering adaptive security responses.

UBA is particularly valuable in detecting insider threats, which pose significant risks to organizations. Unlike external attackers, insiders already have legitimate access to sensitive systems, making their unauthorized activities harder to detect using conventional access control methods. By continuously monitoring access patterns, UBA can recognize subtle changes in user behavior that may indicate malicious intent, data exfiltration, or credential misuse. For example, if an employee who typically accesses customer records during business hours suddenly begins downloading large amounts of data late at night, UBA can flag this activity as suspicious and prompt an access control decision such as denying the request, requiring additional authentication, or alerting security teams.

Compromised accounts are another critical security concern that UBA helps mitigate. Attackers frequently use stolen credentials to bypass traditional access control mechanisms and move laterally within an organization's network. Since stolen credentials appear legitimate, RBAC and ABAC alone cannot distinguish between the real user and an attacker using the same credentials. UBA enhances security by analyzing login behavior, access frequency, and device fingerprinting to detect anomalies that indicate credential compromise. For example, if a user logs in from an IP address in a different country than usual, or if they attempt to access systems they have never used before, UBA can trigger step-up authentication or automatic access revocation.

UBA also plays a crucial role in risk-based access control, where access decisions are dynamically adjusted based on real-time risk assessments. Instead of relying on static access permissions, organizations can implement adaptive security policies that react to behavioral risks. For instance:

A finance employee accessing payroll data from a recognized device and approved location is granted access without friction.

The same employee attempting to access payroll data from an unrecognized device on a public Wi-Fi network triggers a security check that requires multi-factor authentication (MFA).

If the employee further attempts multiple failed login attempts, the system automatically blocks access and alerts the security team.

By integrating UBA with access control systems, organizations can prevent unauthorized access in real time while reducing unnecessary security barriers for legitimate users.

UBA is particularly useful in cloud environments and remote work scenarios, where users access enterprise resources from multiple locations, devices, and networks. Traditional perimeter-based security models are ineffective in these settings, as access control decisions must account for variable risk factors such as device security posture, network trustworthiness, and geolocation. UBA strengthens access control by correlating these risk factors with historical user behavior, allowing for fine-grained access control decisions that continuously adapt to emerging threats.

Behavioral analytics also enhance privileged access management (PAM) by ensuring that administrators and high-risk users do not abuse their privileges. Privileged users, such as system administrators, database managers, and security analysts, often have broad access rights that, if misused, can result in catastrophic data breaches. UBA monitors privileged users for unusual access patterns, unauthorized privilege escalation, and risky operations, triggering automated security responses when necessary.

For example, a system administrator attempting to modify security logs or disable audit trails may indicate an attempt to cover unauthorized actions. UBA can detect such actions and automatically log the event, revoke privileges, or initiate an incident response.

UBA also helps detect slow, stealthy attacks, such as low-and-slow data exfiltration, where an attacker gradually extracts sensitive data over an extended period to evade detection. Traditional security measures may fail to notice such activities because the data volume per request is small. However, UBA can identify deviations from normal access patterns, flagging incremental data transfers as part of a larger malicious activity.

UBA-powered identity analytics can further enhance role-based access reviews by identifying inactive accounts, excessive permissions, and privilege creep. Organizations often struggle with role explosion, where RBAC systems accumulate too many roles, creating unnecessary complexity. UBA helps streamline role management by analyzing how users actually utilize their permissions and recommending role adjustments based on real behavior. For instance:

If an employee is assigned admin privileges but never uses them, UBA can recommend removing or downgrading their role to reduce risk.

If a user has multiple roles with overlapping permissions, UBA can consolidate them to simplify access control policies.

UBA also plays a role in automated incident response by integrating with Security Information and Event Management (SIEM) systems, Endpoint Detection and Response (EDR) platforms, and Identity and Access Management (IAM) solutions. When UBA detects suspicious behavior, it can trigger automated security workflows, such as:

Temporarily locking the user account and requiring security verification.

Revoking session tokens for suspicious activities.

Alerting security analysts for further investigation.

Forcing password resets for compromised accounts.

To successfully implement UBA in access control decisions, organizations must establish a baseline of normal user behavior. This requires collecting and analyzing historical access logs, application usage data, and contextual attributes to create a comprehensive profile of each user's typical activities. Machine learning algorithms refine this baseline over time, improving detection accuracy and reducing false positives.

Organizations adopting UBA must also address privacy and ethical concerns related to continuous monitoring. While UBA enhances security, it must be implemented with clear policies that define what data is collected, how it is used, and how it aligns with compliance requirements such as GDPR and HIPAA. Transparency and user consent are critical in balancing security with employee privacy rights.

UBA is a powerful tool for enhancing access control decisions, bridging the gap between static access models and real-time adaptive security. By continuously analyzing user behavior, access patterns, and contextual risk factors, UBA enables organizations to detect threats proactively, enforce dynamic security measures, and improve access governance. As cyber threats become more sophisticated, the integration of UBA with access control frameworks will be essential for building resilient, intelligent, and risk-aware security architectures.

Future Trends in Access Control

As cybersecurity threats continue to evolve, access control technologies must adapt to meet the growing challenges of securing digital identities, cloud environments, and hybrid infrastructures. Traditional models such as Role-Based Access Control (RBAC) and Attribute-Based Access Control (ABAC) have served as the foundation for identity and access management (IAM), but new advancements in artificial intelligence, behavioral analytics, and decentralized identity are reshaping the future of access control. Emerging trends focus on automation, adaptability, risk-based decision-making, and seamless user experience while maintaining strict security standards.

One of the most significant trends in access control is AI-driven and adaptive access control. Artificial intelligence (AI) and machine learning (ML) are transforming how access decisions are made by incorporating real-time behavioral analysis, threat intelligence, and contextual data. Instead of relying on static rules and predefined attributes, AI-enhanced access control systems continuously learn from user behavior and automatically adjust access permissions based on risk assessments. If an AI-powered system detects an anomalous login attempt, such as access from an unusual geographic location or a sudden request for highly sensitive data, it can trigger step-up authentication, temporary access restrictions, or immediate account suspension to prevent potential security breaches.

Risk-based access control (RBAC, distinct from role-based models) is another growing trend, enabling dynamic security enforcement based on real-time risk scoring. Instead of granting broad access rights based on roles alone, risk-based models analyze multiple risk factors, including device trust, login patterns, and network security posture. For example, an employee accessing company resources from an approved corporate laptop may experience a frictionless login process, while the same employee attempting access from a public Wi-Fi network on an unknown device may be required to provide additional authentication or be denied access entirely. By incorporating risk-aware decision-making, organizations can balance security with usability, reducing unnecessary authentication challenges while mitigating threats.

Zero Trust security models are increasingly shaping the future of access control by enforcing the principle of "never trust, always verify." Instead of relying on perimeter-based defenses, Zero Trust requires continuous verification of identity, device security, and access permissions. Access control solutions are evolving to support continuous authentication, where users are not just authenticated at login but are monitored throughout their session. If an access control system detects a deviation in behavior—such as accessing restricted files outside of business hours or executing unauthorized commands—the system can automatically revalidate the user's identity, enforce step-up authentication, or terminate the session.

Another major advancement in access control is passwordless authentication, which reduces reliance on traditional passwords and enhances security through biometric verification, cryptographic authentication, and hardware security tokens. Multi-factor authentication (MFA) is evolving to become context-aware and adaptive, meaning that authentication requirements change dynamically based on risk factors. Instead of requiring MFA for every login, modern access control systems analyze device reputation, geolocation, and historical behavior to determine when additional authentication is necessary. This approach significantly improves user experience while maintaining strong security controls.

Just-In-Time (JIT) access control is gaining widespread adoption, particularly in cloud environments, DevOps workflows, and privileged access management (PAM). Traditional access control models often grant excessive, long-term permissions, increasing the risk of privilege misuse and insider threats. JIT access ensures that users receive only the permissions they need, when they need them, and for a limited time. For example, a cloud administrator requiring elevated privileges to perform a critical system update would request temporary access, with permissions automatically revoked once the task is completed. This approach aligns with Zero Standing Privileges (ZSP), ensuring that no user has permanent administrative access unless explicitly required.

The rise of decentralized identity and blockchain-based access control is transforming how digital identities are managed. Traditional IAM systems rely on centralized identity providers (IdPs) such as corporate directories or cloud-based authentication services. However, decentralized identity frameworks, powered by blockchain technology, allow users to own and control their digital identities without relying on third-party providers. In decentralized access control models, individuals can authenticate themselves using verifiable credentials stored on a blockchain, ensuring greater privacy, security, and resistance to identity theft. This trend is particularly relevant for cross-organization and federated access management, where users need secure access to multiple systems across different enterprises without relying on a central authority.

Federated access control and cross-cloud IAM integration are becoming increasingly important as organizations expand into multi-cloud environments. Managing user access across multiple cloud providers—such as AWS, Microsoft Azure, and Google Cloud—requires a unified identity governance strategy. Federated identity solutions allow users to authenticate seamlessly across different cloud platforms while maintaining consistent access policies. This ensures that organizations can enforce uniform security controls regardless of where applications and data are hosted.

Quantum computing is expected to impact access control in the near future, necessitating the development of quantum-resistant authentication and encryption techniques. Traditional encryption methods that protect passwords, digital certificates, and identity tokens may become vulnerable to quantum attacks. Organizations are already exploring post-quantum cryptographic algorithms to safeguard access control mechanisms against emerging threats. In response, next-generation access control systems will incorporate quantum-safe authentication to ensure that digital identities remain secure in a post-quantum world.

The increasing reliance on identity threat detection and response (ITDR) is another key trend shaping the future of access control. As cybercriminals continue to exploit stolen credentials, phishing attacks, and social engineering, organizations must adopt proactive identity security measures. ITDR solutions integrate with access control systems, SIEM platforms, and behavioral analytics tools to detect identity-based threats in real time. When suspicious activities are detected—such as unauthorized privilege escalation or anomalous access requests—ITDR solutions trigger automated security responses, including revoking access, forcing identity re-verification, or quarantining compromised accounts.

Automation and AI-driven policy orchestration are also transforming how access control policies are created, managed, and enforced. Traditional access control systems require manual policy configurations, making them complex and difficult to scale. AI-powered access control solutions analyze user behavior, organizational workflows, and historical access trends to recommend optimized policies that improve security while reducing administrative overhead. These solutions can automatically detect excessive permissions, role conflicts, and outdated policies, ensuring that access control remains efficient, adaptive, and continuously refined.

The future of access control is defined by intelligent automation, continuous authentication, and risk-adaptive decision-making. Organizations are moving toward dynamic, real-time access control models that integrate AI, behavioral analytics, and decentralized identity frameworks to create frictionless yet highly secure access environments. As cyber threats continue to evolve, access control solutions must remain flexible, scalable, and resilient, ensuring that users, applications, and systems are protected from unauthorized access while maintaining seamless digital experiences.

Implementing RBAC/ABAC in Large Organizations

Implementing Role-Based Access Control (RBAC) and Attribute-Based Access Control (ABAC) in large organizations requires a strategic, scalable, and well-governed approach. Large enterprises face complex access control challenges due to their diverse workforce, multiple business units, global operations, regulatory requirements, and rapidly changing IT environments. While RBAC provides a structured, role-driven access model, ABAC introduces dynamic and context-aware policies, making it essential for organizations to integrate both models to achieve scalability, flexibility, and security.

One of the first steps in implementing RBAC and ABAC in large organizations is conducting an access control audit to understand existing roles, permissions, access patterns, and potential security risks. Many organizations suffer from role explosion, where excessive and overlapping roles create administrative complexity and security gaps. A role cleanup process is necessary to eliminate redundant roles, consolidate permissions, and define clear role hierarchies.

RBAC implementation begins with defining core business roles based on job functions, responsibilities, and departments. Roles such as Finance Analyst, HR Manager, IT Administrator, and Sales Representative should have predefined permissions aligned with job duties. Organizations should follow the principle of least privilege, ensuring that users are granted only the minimum access necessary to perform their tasks.

ABAC enhances RBAC by introducing real-time attributes to refine access decisions. Instead of granting static permissions based solely on roles, ABAC evaluates user attributes (e.g., job title, security clearance, employment status), resource attributes (e.g., document classification, data sensitivity), and contextual attributes (e.g., time of access, device trustworthiness, network location). This dynamic policy enforcement ensures that access control decisions are continuously updated based on changing risk conditions.

A large-scale RBAC/ABAC implementation requires centralized identity governance and policy management. Enterprises should deploy an Identity and Access Management (IAM) solution that integrates with Active Directory (AD), LDAP, Single Sign-On (SSO), and cloud identity providers. A centralized IAM system allows organizations to automate user provisioning, enforce role-based policies, and manage attribute synchronization across multiple applications.

Access certification and periodic reviews are crucial for maintaining role integrity and policy effectiveness. Large organizations often experience role drift, where users accumulate excessive permissions over time due to organizational changes, promotions, or temporary access grants. IAM platforms provide automated access review workflows, allowing managers and security teams to validate role assignments, revoke unnecessary access, and ensure compliance with security policies.

Integrating RBAC and ABAC requires a policy definition framework that supports both static and dynamic access control. For example, a hybrid policy might state:

RBAC rule: "A Finance Analyst can access financial reports."

ABAC refinement: "Access is granted only during business hours and only if the request originates from a corporate-managed device."

This hybrid approach reduces excessive permissions while ensuring that access is contextually appropriate.

In multi-cloud and hybrid environments, RBAC and ABAC policies must be consistently enforced across AWS, Azure, Google Cloud, and on-premises systems. Cloud platforms offer built-in role-based access management (RBAC), but large organizations must extend ABAC policies to evaluate real-time security conditions such as:

Device compliance (e.g., has the latest security patches been applied?).

Geographic restrictions (e.g., block access from high-risk countries).

Behavioral analytics (e.g., is the user accessing resources in an unusual pattern?).

Privileged Access Management (PAM) is another essential component of RBAC/ABAC deployment in large organizations. IT administrators, DevOps engineers, and security teams require elevated access to critical systems, but granting permanent privileges increases the risk of insider threats and credential misuse. Just-In-Time (JIT) access control should be implemented to grant temporary, time-bound privileges only when needed. For example:

A cloud engineer can request administrative access for 1 hour to modify a production server.

An IT support technician can access sensitive logs only after managerial approval.

This model, combined with Zero Standing Privileges (ZSP), ensures that no privileged account retains unnecessary long-term access.

Large organizations must also address compliance and regulatory requirements, including GDPR, HIPAA, SOX, and ISO 27001. RBAC simplifies compliance reporting by providing structured access hierarchies, while ABAC enforces dynamic risk-based access control policies to meet data protection regulations.

Auditability is critical for tracking access control decisions, policy changes, and security incidents. Security teams should integrate RBAC/ABAC policies with Security Information and Event Management (SIEM) solutions to monitor access logs, detect anomalies, and respond to potential breaches.

Automating RBAC/ABAC policy enforcement reduces administrative burden and improves access control efficiency. AI-driven identity governance solutions can analyze user behavior, access history, and policy violations to recommend role adjustments, policy refinements, and security improvements.

For successful implementation, training and awareness programs must be established to educate employees on access control policies, data protection best practices, and compliance requirements. Security teams should regularly conduct RBAC/ABAC audits, access control simulations, and penetration testing to identify gaps, misconfigurations, or role abuses.

By integrating RBAC's structured role management with ABAC's dynamic and contextual access policies, large organizations can build a scalable, secure, and adaptable access control framework that meets evolving security needs while ensuring regulatory compliance, operational efficiency, and reduced insider threats.

Common Pitfalls and How to Avoid Them

Implementing access control frameworks such as Role-Based Access Control (RBAC) and Attribute-Based Access Control (ABAC) presents numerous challenges, particularly in large organizations. While these models enhance security and governance, they are often prone to misconfigurations, administrative burdens, and security gaps when not properly planned. Organizations that fail to address common pitfalls risk privilege escalation, role explosion, excessive permissions, and compliance violations. Understanding these pitfalls and how to mitigate them is essential for maintaining a secure and scalable access control system.

One of the most significant pitfalls in access control implementation is role explosion in RBAC. Organizations often create too many roles to accommodate granular access needs, leading to complexity, redundancy, and administrative overhead. Instead of simplifying access management, role explosion results in an unmanageable number of roles, making it difficult to audit and maintain security policies. To avoid this, organizations should:

Follow a role minimization strategy, grouping users with similar responsibilities under broader roles.

Implement role hierarchies to inherit permissions instead of duplicating roles.

Use ABAC to refine RBAC policies, allowing attributes such as department, security level, and location to dynamically adjust access rather than creating separate roles for each condition.

Another common issue is excessive permissions, where users are granted more access than necessary for their job functions. This problem is often due to permission creep, where users accumulate access rights over time without revoking outdated privileges. Excessive permissions increase the risk of insider threats and data breaches. Organizations can mitigate this by:

Enforcing the principle of least privilege (PoLP) to ensure that users have only the minimum access required.

Conducting periodic access reviews and role recertification to identify and remove unnecessary permissions.

Implementing Just-In-Time (JIT) access to grant temporary privileges only when needed instead of permanent permissions.

Another pitfall is over-reliance on static access control models. While RBAC is effective for structured role management, it lacks the flexibility needed for modern cloud and hybrid environments. Many organizations implement RBAC without considering the need for dynamic, real-time access decisions. This can lead to security gaps where users retain access rights under outdated conditions. To avoid this, organizations should:

Combine RBAC with ABAC to introduce dynamic access control based on contextual attributes.

Use risk-based access control (RBAC) mechanisms to evaluate real-time factors such as device security, user behavior, and network trust level.

Adopt adaptive access control strategies, where permissions adjust based on security conditions and access history.

Poorly defined role hierarchies and policy inconsistencies also create major access control challenges. In large organizations, different business units may develop inconsistent access policies, leading to conflicts, misconfigurations, and security gaps. A user in one department may have different access policies than an equivalent user in another department, causing confusion and compliance risks. To prevent this:

Standardize access control policies across all departments to ensure consistency.

Define clear access control governance with centralized policy management and enforcement.

Use automation and identity governance tools to enforce role and attribute consistency across the organization.

Another frequent issue is failure to properly manage attribute sources in ABAC. ABAC relies on real-time attributes such as user role, department, location, device security posture, and risk score. However, if attributes are incomplete, outdated, or inconsistent, access control decisions may be incorrect, leading to unauthorized access or unintended restrictions. To address this, organizations should:

Ensure attribute data is accurate and continuously updated by integrating access control with identity management systems, HR databases, and security monitoring tools.

Use attribute validation mechanisms to prevent stale or misconfigured attribute values from affecting access decisions.

Automate attribute synchronization across multiple systems to maintain consistency.

Lack of proper access auditing and monitoring is another pitfall that can lead to undetected security threats. Organizations that fail to monitor access logs, detect anomalies, and enforce logging mechanisms may be unable to track unauthorized access or privilege abuse. This lack of visibility can result in data breaches, regulatory violations, and insider threats going unnoticed. To improve auditing and monitoring:

Integrate access control systems with Security Information and Event Management (SIEM) tools to detect suspicious access patterns.

Implement user behavior analytics (UBA) to identify anomalies in access requests.

Conduct regular access control audits to validate policy effectiveness and detect potential security issues.

Another common mistake is failing to enforce multi-factor authentication (MFA) for high-risk access. Many organizations implement RBAC and ABAC but do not strengthen authentication requirements, making privileged accounts susceptible to credential theft and brute-force attacks. To enhance security:

Require MFA for all privileged access, remote access, and access to sensitive data.

Implement adaptive authentication, where additional verification is required based on real-time risk assessments.

Use passwordless authentication mechanisms, such as biometric authentication or security keys, to reduce reliance on traditional passwords.

Lack of user training and awareness is another major issue that leads to misuse of access privileges. Even with robust access control models, security is compromised when users share credentials, fall victim to phishing attacks, or bypass security controls. To address this:

Provide regular security awareness training on access control policies and best practices.

Educate employees on the risks of privilege misuse and unauthorized access.

Implement user-friendly access request and approval workflows to discourage users from seeking unauthorized workarounds.

Finally, a significant pitfall in access control implementation is neglecting scalability and automation. Many organizations hard-code access policies into applications, making them difficult to scale as the business grows. Manual access control processes increase administrative burden and delay access approvals, leading to operational inefficiencies. To avoid this:

Use policy orchestration and automated role assignments to scale access control dynamically.

Leverage AI-driven identity governance to detect excessive permissions and recommend optimized policies.

Implement centralized access management solutions that integrate with cloud environments, SaaS applications, and hybrid infrastructures.

By proactively addressing these common pitfalls, organizations can create a secure, efficient, and scalable access control system that enhances security while reducing administrative complexity, minimizing risks, and ensuring compliance.

Security and Compliance Regulations Impacting Access Control

Security and compliance regulations play a critical role in shaping access control policies for organizations worldwide. As businesses handle sensitive data, including personally identifiable information (PII), financial records, and healthcare information, they must comply with a variety of legal and industry-specific requirements to protect data from unauthorized access, breaches, and misuse. Regulations dictate how organizations implement access control frameworks such as Role-Based Access Control (RBAC) and Attribute-Based Access Control (ABAC) to enforce security measures, ensure proper user authentication, and prevent unauthorized access to sensitive systems and data.

One of the most well-known regulations impacting access control is the General Data Protection Regulation (GDPR), which governs data protection and privacy for individuals in the European Union (EU). GDPR requires organizations to implement strict access controls to protect personal data from unauthorized processing, disclosure, or loss. Under GDPR, organizations must enforce least privilege access, meaning that employees and third parties can only access data necessary for their job functions. GDPR also mandates data access logs and audit trails, ensuring that organizations can monitor and track who accessed personal data and when. Failure to comply with GDPR can lead to severe penalties, including fines of up to €20 million or 4% of annual global turnover, whichever is higher.

In the healthcare sector, the Health Insurance Portability and Accountability Act (HIPAA) establishes strict access control requirements for protecting patient health information (PHI). HIPAA mandates that healthcare providers, insurance companies, and business associates implement technical safeguards such as unique user identification, role-based access control, audit logging, and automatic session termination to prevent unauthorized access to electronic health records (EHRs). Healthcare organizations must enforce access control mechanisms that limit PHI exposure based on job roles, ensuring that only authorized personnel can access patient data for legitimate treatment, payment, or operational purposes.

Financial institutions must comply with Sarbanes-Oxley Act (SOX) regulations, which were enacted to prevent corporate fraud and protect financial data integrity. SOX requires organizations to maintain strict internal controls over financial reporting (ICFR), including access control policies that limit who can modify or access financial systems and records. Organizations must implement user authentication, role-based access permissions, and audit trails to ensure that financial data cannot be altered or accessed without proper authorization. Failure to comply with SOX can result in legal penalties, financial fines, and reputational damage.

For organizations handling payment transactions, the Payment Card Industry Data Security Standard (PCI DSS) establishes security standards to protect credit card data. PCI DSS requires businesses to implement access control mechanisms that restrict access to cardholder data on a need-to-know basis. Organizations must enforce multi-factor authentication (MFA) for accessing payment systems, regularly review access permissions, and monitor all user activities to detect unauthorized access attempts. PCI DSS compliance is essential for merchants, payment processors, and financial institutions to reduce the risk of fraud, data breaches, and cyberattacks targeting payment data.

In the government and defense sectors, NIST Special Publication 800-53 outlines security and privacy controls for federal agencies and contractors handling government information. NIST 800-53 includes stringent access control requirements such as role-based and attribute-based access control, identity verification, and continuous monitoring to prevent unauthorized data access. Federal agencies must also comply with the Federal Information Security Modernization Act (FISMA), which mandates strict security policies to protect government systems and classified information.

Organizations operating in multiple jurisdictions often face challenges complying with overlapping security regulations that impose different access control requirements. For example, a multinational corporation may need to comply with GDPR in Europe, HIPAA in the United States, and ISO/IEC 27001 in global operations. To streamline compliance, organizations must adopt a unified access control strategy that integrates identity and access management (IAM) solutions with automated policy enforcement.

Zero Trust security frameworks are gaining prominence as organizations align access control policies with compliance requirements. Zero Trust enforces continuous identity verification, least privilege access, and contextual risk assessments to comply with regulations such as CMMC (Cybersecurity Maturity Model Certification) for defense contractors and NYDFS Cybersecurity Regulation for financial institutions.

To ensure regulatory compliance, organizations must implement automated access governance tools that provide real-time visibility into user permissions, role assignments, and access logs. These tools help organizations enforce policy-based access control (PBAC) that dynamically adjusts access permissions based on compliance requirements and business needs.

Access control audits are essential for regulatory compliance, enabling organizations to verify that users have appropriate access levels and that security policies are being enforced consistently. Regulatory audits often require organizations to generate detailed access reports, incident logs, and policy enforcement records to demonstrate compliance with data protection laws.

Organizations should adopt a proactive approach to compliance by regularly reviewing access control policies, conducting penetration tests, and implementing automated compliance monitoring tools. By aligning access control strategies with regulatory frameworks, organizations can reduce security risks, protect sensitive data, and avoid costly penalties associated with non-compliance.

Access Control in DevOps and CI/CD Pipelines

Access control in DevOps and Continuous Integration/Continuous Deployment (CI/CD) pipelines is a critical aspect of securing software development environments. Modern DevOps practices emphasize automation, rapid deployment, and cloud-based infrastructure, creating security challenges that traditional access control models struggle to address. Developers, testers, system administrators, and automated processes all require different levels of access to source code repositories, build systems, and deployment environments. Without a robust access control strategy, organizations risk privilege misuse, unauthorized code changes, security misconfigurations, and insider threats.

DevOps workflows operate in highly dynamic environments where infrastructure, code, and configurations change frequently. Traditional access control models such as Role-Based Access Control (RBAC) alone are insufficient because they rely on static role assignments that do not adapt to real-time security conditions. Instead, a combination of RBAC, Attribute-Based Access Control (ABAC), and Just-In-Time (JIT) access control is needed to enforce dynamic, least-privilege access policies that accommodate the speed and flexibility of DevOps pipelines.

One of the key access control challenges in DevOps is securing source code repositories. Platforms such as GitHub, GitLab, and Bitbucket require strict access policies to prevent unauthorized code modifications, repository cloning, and privilege escalation. Organizations should enforce fine-grained access controls based on roles and contextual attributes. For example, a developer may be granted read and write access to their project repositories but restricted from merging code into the main branch without approval. Security teams should also enforce multi-factor authentication (MFA), branch protection rules, and access audits to reduce the risk of unauthorized commits and accidental credential leaks.

Another critical aspect of access control in DevOps is managing credentials and secrets used in CI/CD pipelines. Automated build and deployment processes often require access to cloud services, databases, and infrastructure components, which means storing API keys, SSH credentials, and service tokens securely. Hardcoding credentials into configuration files or CI/CD scripts poses a significant security risk, as attackers can easily extract them if the repository is compromised. Organizations should use secrets management solutions such as HashiCorp Vault, AWS Secrets Manager, and Azure Key Vault to securely store and inject secrets into pipelines at runtime instead of embedding them in code.

Securing CI/CD pipelines is another fundamental challenge. Build automation tools such as Jenkins, GitHub Actions, GitLab CI, and Azure DevOps require controlled access to code repositories, build artifacts, and deployment environments. Organizations should enforce least-privilege access by ensuring that:

CI/CD runners and build agents only have access to necessary repositories and credentials.

Build processes run in isolated environments with temporary access tokens instead of persistent credentials.

Access to production environments is restricted and requires manual approval or Just-In-Time (JIT) access.

One of the biggest security risks in DevOps is privilege escalation through misconfigured CI/CD permissions. Attackers can exploit improperly configured pipeline permissions to execute malicious code or gain access to sensitive data. Organizations should implement role-based and attribute-based policies that enforce security checks before executing privileged actions such as infrastructure provisioning, container deployments, and system modifications.

Cloud environments play a crucial role in modern DevOps, requiring cloud-native access control policies. DevOps teams frequently use Infrastructure as Code (IaC) tools such as Terraform, Ansible, and CloudFormation to provision cloud resources. Misconfigurations in IAM roles, security groups, and access policies can expose cloud workloads to unauthorized access, data leaks, and privilege escalation attacks. Organizations should enforce least-privilege IAM policies by:

Defining role-based access policies that restrict who can provision, modify, and delete cloud resources.

Applying attribute-based policies to limit access based on contextual factors such as geolocation, device security, and time of access.

Enforcing multi-factor authentication (MFA) for all privileged access to cloud environments.

Securing containerized applications and Kubernetes clusters is another critical area of DevOps access control. Kubernetes clusters typically have multiple layers of access control, including role-based access control (RBAC), namespace isolation, and network security policies. Organizations should:

Implement Kubernetes RBAC to define role-based access to cluster resources, restricting who can create, delete, or modify containers.

Use attribute-based policies to enforce security conditions such as requiring workloads to run in specific namespaces or ensuring that only trusted container images are deployed.

Integrate Kubernetes with IAM solutions to enforce unified authentication and authorization across cloud and on-prem environments.

Just-In-Time (JIT) access control plays a significant role in securing DevOps workflows by eliminating persistent privileges. Instead of granting long-term admin access, DevOps engineers should be able to request temporary elevated privileges only when required. This ensures that privileged actions are logged, monitored, and automatically revoked after a predefined period, reducing the risk of credential misuse and privilege escalation attacks.

Auditability and real-time monitoring are essential components of access control in DevOps environments. Organizations must track all access events, permission changes, and security violations within their pipelines. Security teams should:

Integrate DevOps access control logs with SIEM (Security Information and Event Management) tools to detect anomalies.

Use User Behavior Analytics (UBA) to monitor access patterns and flag suspicious activity.

Conduct regular access reviews and automated compliance checks to ensure that access policies remain aligned with security best practices.

DevSecOps, the practice of integrating security into DevOps processes, emphasizes proactive access control measures to reduce vulnerabilities in CI/CD pipelines. By embedding security controls early in the software development lifecycle (SDLC), organizations can:

Implement static and dynamic code analysis to identify security risks before deployment.

Enforce automated security scans in CI/CD pipelines to detect misconfigurations and vulnerabilities.

Adopt a Zero Trust security model that continuously validates identities, device security, and workload behavior.

Access control in DevOps and CI/CD pipelines requires a multi-layered security strategy that combines role-based governance, dynamic attribute-based policies, secrets management, and real-time monitoring. Organizations that enforce least privilege access, automate security checks, and integrate identity governance tools will significantly reduce the risk of privilege abuse, misconfigurations, and unauthorized access in their software development lifecycle.

RBAC/ABAC in Financial and Healthcare Sectors

The financial and healthcare sectors handle highly sensitive data, making robust access control mechanisms essential to prevent unauthorized access, data breaches, and regulatory violations. Both industries must comply with strict security standards and regulatory frameworks such as GDPR, HIPAA, SOX, and PCI DSS, which mandate strong authentication, least privilege access, and detailed audit trails. Traditional Role Based Access Control (RBAC) has been widely adopted in these industries due to its structured approach to permission management, but it often lacks the flexibility required for modern, dynamic environments. Attribute-Based Access Control (ABAC) enhances security by incorporating real-time attributes such as device security posture, location, and risk level to make context-aware access decisions.

In the financial sector, institutions such as banks, investment firms, and insurance companies manage high-value transactions, customer financial records, and regulatory reports. Unauthorized access to financial data can lead to fraud, money laundering, insider trading, and reputational damage. RBAC is commonly used to define access permissions based on job roles such as Teller, Loan Officer, Financial Analyst, and Risk Manager. Each role has predefined access to customer accounts, transaction systems, and financial reports, ensuring that employees can only access data relevant to their job function.

However, RBAC alone is insufficient to handle real-time fraud detection, dynamic risk assessments, and regulatory compliance. ABAC enhances RBAC by introducing attribute-based conditions that refine access permissions based on security context. For example, an ABAC policy in a bank may enforce:

A loan officer can access customer financial data only if the customer has an active loan application and the request is made from a secure company-managed device.

A trader can execute transactions only if they have completed mandatory compliance training and are operating within regulatory limits.

A finance executive can approve wire transfers only if the transaction does not exceed predefined risk thresholds and has been approved by a secondary reviewer.

The combination of RBAC and ABAC ensures that financial institutions enforce risk-based access controls, reducing exposure to insider threats and fraudulent activities while maintaining operational efficiency.

The healthcare sector also relies on RBAC and ABAC to protect electronic health records (EHRs), medical billing data, and patient treatment histories. Unauthorized access to healthcare data can lead to identity theft, insurance fraud, and regulatory penalties under HIPAA and GDPR. RBAC is commonly used to assign access permissions to roles such as Doctor, Nurse, Pharmacist, and Medical Billing Specialist.

For example, a doctor may have full access to a patient's medical history, while a nurse may only access treatment notes and a pharmacist may only view prescription records. This structured approach ensures that healthcare professionals can access necessary patient information while preventing overexposure to sensitive data.

However, RBAC alone cannot accommodate the complexity of modern healthcare workflows, where access needs to be dynamic, patient-centric, and risk-aware. ABAC enhances access control by enforcing contextual conditions such as:

A doctor can access a patient's full medical record only if they are actively treating the patient and the request is made within a hospital network.

A nurse can update medication schedules only if they are on duty and assigned to the patient's care team.

An insurance auditor can review billing records only if the patient has provided explicit consent and the request is within the allowable audit period.

Emergency access policies, also known as break-glass scenarios, are critical in healthcare settings. ABAC can dynamically grant temporary access overrides in life-threatening situations while ensuring that all emergency access events are logged and reviewed. For example, if an unconscious patient arrives in the emergency room, an ABAC policy may temporarily allow any attending physician to access the patient's medical history without prior authorization. Once the emergency is resolved, access permissions revert to their original state.

Both financial and healthcare organizations must comply with strict regulatory requirements, making access control auditability and compliance enforcement essential. Regulatory frameworks such as SOX (Sarbanes-Oxley Act) in finance and HIPAA (Health Insurance Portability and Accountability Act) in healthcare require organizations to:

Maintain detailed access logs that track who accessed what data, when, and why.

Enforce multi-factor authentication (MFA) for privileged access to sensitive systems.

Conduct regular access reviews to ensure that users retain only necessary permissions.

Implement segregation of duties (SoD) to prevent conflicts of interest, such as a finance employee who approves transactions also having access to modify accounting records.

RBAC and ABAC enhance compliance efforts by providing structured role definitions, dynamic attribute-based policies, and real-time access monitoring. Financial institutions can use RBAC to assign permissions based on job functions and ABAC to refine access based on transaction risk levels and compliance status. Similarly, healthcare providers can use RBAC to enforce professional access boundaries and ABAC to introduce patient-centric and time-sensitive access conditions.

Access control automation and policy orchestration are becoming essential in financial and healthcare organizations to reduce administrative burden and improve security enforcement. Identity Governance and Administration (IGA) tools help organizations:

Automate role assignments based on job function, reducing manual errors.

Enforce least privilege access dynamically using risk-based ABAC policies.

Integrate with Security Information and Event Management (SIEM) systems to detect and respond to unauthorized access attempts.

The financial and healthcare sectors are also adopting Zero Trust security models, which eliminate implicit trust and continuously verify user identities and security conditions. Zero Trust enforces:

Just-In-Time (JIT) access, where privileges are granted temporarily and revoked once the task is complete.

Continuous authentication, ensuring that users maintain access only if their behavior remains consistent with expected patterns.

Real-time risk assessments, adjusting access permissions dynamically based on security posture.

As financial and healthcare organizations continue to digitize their operations and adopt cloud-based systems, RBAC and ABAC must evolve to support hybrid IT environments, federated identity management, and AI-driven access control policies. By integrating role-based governance with dynamic attribute-based access rules, organizations can enforce scalable, secure, and compliance-ready access control frameworks that protect sensitive financial and medical data.

Access Control Testing and Validation Strategies

Access control testing and validation are essential components of a secure identity and access management (IAM) framework. Without proper testing, misconfigurations and vulnerabilities can lead to unauthorized access, data breaches, and regulatory violations. Organizations implementing Role-Based Access Control (RBAC) and Attribute-Based Access Control (ABAC) must conduct rigorous validation to ensure that access policies enforce least privilege, segregation of duties (SoD), and compliance with security regulations.

Effective access control testing involves evaluating authentication mechanisms, authorization policies, privilege escalation risks, and auditing capabilities. The goal is to verify that users have appropriate access, detect excessive permissions, and prevent unauthorized privilege assignments. By implementing structured testing methodologies, organizations can identify security gaps before attackers exploit them.

One of the foundational access control validation strategies is role and permission reviews. In organizations using RBAC, access control tests should evaluate whether users are assigned to the correct roles and whether roles are properly defined. Common testing steps include:

Verifying that role assignments align with job functions and do not exceed necessary permissions.

Identifying orphaned roles and inactive accounts that may still have access to sensitive systems.

Checking for role conflicts and segregation of duties (SoD) violations, such as users who can both approve and execute financial transactions, which creates a fraud risk.

Automated access certification reviews streamline these audits by periodically prompting managers and security teams to review user access, approve necessary permissions, and revoke excessive privileges.

For ABAC implementations, attribute validation testing ensures that dynamic access control policies enforce security conditions correctly. ABAC policies rely on attributes such as user identity, device security posture, location, and behavioral risk scores to determine access. Key testing strategies include:

Simulating different attribute values to verify that policies enforce correct access decisions.

Checking for inconsistencies in attribute sources, ensuring that identity providers, HR systems, and security monitoring tools provide accurate attribute data.

Testing real-time enforcement of contextual access restrictions, such as denying access if a request comes from an untrusted network or requiring additional authentication for high-risk actions.

One of the most important security testing strategies is penetration testing (pen testing) and ethical hacking. Security teams and third-party auditors conduct penetration tests to simulate real-world attack scenarios and identify access control vulnerabilities. Common pen testing methods include:

Privilege escalation testing, where testers attempt to gain unauthorized administrative privileges through misconfigured role assignments or system flaws.

Bypassing authentication mechanisms, such as testing for weak passwords, MFA misconfigurations, or session hijacking vulnerabilities.

Exploiting misconfigured access control policies, such as attempting unauthorized API calls, database queries, or file access.

Penetration tests uncover access control weaknesses that traditional policy reviews may overlook, helping organizations strengthen defenses before malicious actors can exploit them.

Dynamic access control testing is another critical validation strategy. Unlike static role-based models, modern access control frameworks must support adaptive security policies that react to real-time conditions. Security teams can conduct real-time access simulations to validate dynamic policy enforcement, including:

Testing risk-based access policies, where access is granted or denied based on user behavior, device security, and contextual risk levels.

Evaluating Just-In-Time (JIT) access scenarios, where users request temporary privileged access, and the system enforces automatic expiration.

Simulating behavioral anomalies, such as logging in from an unusual geographic location, to verify if the system prompts for additional authentication or denies access.

Organizations must also test audit logging and compliance reporting capabilities. Access logs are crucial for forensic investigations, compliance audits, and security monitoring. Key validation steps include:

Ensuring that all access control events are logged and include details such as user identity, accessed resource, timestamp, and access decision.

Verifying that log retention policies comply with industry regulations, such as HIPAA, GDPR, and SOX.

Testing access log integrity, ensuring that privileged users cannot tamper with or delete audit logs to cover unauthorized activities.

Another effective validation method is policy enforcement testing using automated tools. Organizations can leverage access control validation frameworks to test policies against predefined security rules. Tools such as:

IAM policy simulators (e.g., AWS IAM Policy Simulator, Azure Policy Tester) allow security teams to evaluate access policies before deploying them.

Identity governance solutions provide role mining capabilities, helping organizations detect excessive permissions and unnecessary access assignments.

User behavior analytics (UBA) tools monitor access anomalies, privilege misuse, and unauthorized activity patterns in real-time.

Security teams should conduct regression testing after every policy update to ensure that changes do not introduce new vulnerabilities. For example, adding a new role or modifying an ABAC rule may unintentionally grant excessive permissions, which must be detected before the policy is applied to production environments.

Organizations operating in cloud and hybrid environments must conduct cross-platform access control testing. Cloud service providers (CSPs) offer built-in access management controls, but security teams must ensure that policies are enforced consistently across multiple cloud platforms and on-prem systems. Key testing steps include:

Ensuring consistent IAM policies across AWS, Azure, and Google Cloud, preventing misalignment between different platforms.

Validating federated identity access controls, ensuring that Single Sign-On (SSO) and multi-cloud authentication systems enforce uniform access policies.

Simulating cloud access control breaches, such as testing if unauthorized users can access cloud storage, databases, or APIs.

Finally, organizations should implement continuous access monitoring and validation strategies. Security policies and access control configurations should not be one-time implementations but regularly evaluated and improved. This includes:

Conducting automated access recertification every 3–6 months.

Reviewing access logs for abnormal patterns and integrating real-time alerting systems.

Testing policy effectiveness against emerging security threats, ensuring that access control remains aligned with evolving cybersecurity challenges.

Access control testing and validation are essential for maintaining secure, compliant, and resilient access management frameworks. By incorporating regular audits, penetration tests, real-time access simulations, and automated validation tools, organizations can ensure that RBAC, ABAC, and dynamic access policies effectively protect sensitive resources from unauthorized access.

Governance, Risk, and Compliance (GRC) in RBAC/ABAC

Governance, Risk, and Compliance (GRC) is a critical framework for organizations implementing Role-Based Access Control (RBAC) and Attribute-Based Access Control (ABAC). Proper GRC practices ensure that access control policies align with regulatory requirements, security standards, and business objectives while managing risks effectively. Without a structured GRC approach, organizations face challenges such as excessive permissions, compliance violations, insider threats, and unauthorized data access.

Governance in access control refers to establishing policies, defining roles and responsibilities, and enforcing security standards to ensure that access rights are properly managed. Organizations implementing RBAC must define clear role hierarchies, role-based permissions, and segregation of duties (SoD) policies to prevent conflicts of interest. A well-governed RBAC system ensures that employees, contractors, and third parties have access only to the resources necessary for their job functions.

ABAC governance expands upon RBAC by introducing context-aware policies that evaluate real-time attributes such as user location, device security posture, and access history. Organizations must establish governance structures that ensure attribute data sources remain accurate, synchronized, and trustworthy. Without proper governance, outdated or misconfigured attributes may lead to incorrect access decisions and security gaps.

Risk management in RBAC and ABAC involves identifying, analyzing, and mitigating access control risks. Organizations must assess risks related to privileged access, third-party access, insider threats, and compliance misalignment. A common risk in RBAC is role explosion, where too many roles create administrative complexity and security vulnerabilities. Organizations must regularly conduct role mining and optimization to streamline role assignments and prevent privilege creep.

ABAC introduces additional risk factors, particularly in dynamic access control environments where real-time policy enforcement depends on contextual attributes. A key risk is attribute misconfiguration, where incorrect or outdated attribute values may unintentionally grant or deny access. Organizations should implement automated risk assessments and continuous monitoring tools to detect anomalous access patterns and policy inconsistencies.

Compliance is a major driver for organizations implementing RBAC and ABAC. Many industries are subject to strict regulatory frameworks that mandate strong access control mechanisms, auditability, and least privilege enforcement. Regulations such as GDPR, HIPAA, SOX, PCI DSS, and ISO 27001 require organizations to maintain detailed access logs, conduct regular access reviews, and enforce multi-factor authentication (MFA) for sensitive systems.

RBAC simplifies compliance efforts by defining structured access policies that auditors can easily review. Organizations can demonstrate compliance by showing that roles are assigned based on job functions and that no user has excessive permissions beyond their responsibilities. However, RBAC alone is insufficient for dynamic access control needs, particularly in cloud and hybrid environments where access must adapt to real-time risk conditions.

ABAC enhances compliance by introducing fine-grained access policies that dynamically enforce regulatory requirements. For example, an ABAC policy in a financial institution may restrict access to customer financial data based on geolocation, transaction amount, and security clearance level. In a healthcare setting, ABAC can enforce HIPAA-compliant access controls by ensuring that medical records are accessible only to authorized healthcare professionals with an active treatment relationship with the patient.

A key component of access control compliance is auditability and access certification. Organizations must regularly review who has access to what systems, whether access is justified, and whether permissions align with security policies. Automated access certification workflows allow managers to review employee, contractor, and third-party access rights on a scheduled basis, ensuring that excessive or unnecessary privileges are revoked.

Security Information and Event Management (SIEM) tools play a crucial role in monitoring access control compliance. By integrating RBAC and ABAC policies with SIEM solutions, organizations can detect unauthorized access attempts, generate compliance reports, and respond to security incidents in real time.

Another critical aspect of GRC in RBAC and ABAC is segregation of duties (SoD), which prevents conflicts of interest and fraud. In financial institutions, for example, an employee who initiates financial transactions should not have the ability to approve them. SoD policies enforce strict separation between critical business functions, ensuring that no single individual has unchecked control over sensitive operations.

Organizations implementing ABAC must also define clear attribute governance policies to maintain consistent and reliable access decisions. This includes establishing attribute data sources, ensuring real-time synchronization, and preventing stale or inaccurate data from affecting access control enforcement.

Risk-based access control (RBAC) is an emerging trend that integrates real-time risk scoring into access control policies. By combining behavioral analytics, threat intelligence, and AI-driven risk assessments, organizations can dynamically adjust permissions based on evolving security conditions. For example, if a user typically accesses corporate systems from an office location but suddenly logs in from an unknown country, the system can trigger adaptive authentication measures, restrict access, or require additional approvals.

To maintain effective GRC practices in RBAC and ABAC implementations, organizations should adopt automated identity governance solutions that provide continuous access monitoring, role optimization, and compliance reporting. Identity Governance and Administration (IGA) platforms allow organizations to centrally manage access policies, enforce role-based governance, and detect excessive permissions before they become security risks.

A successful GRC strategy in RBAC and ABAC requires a cross-functional collaboration between security teams, compliance officers, IT administrators, and business stakeholders. Organizations should establish governance committees responsible for:

Defining and reviewing access control policies.

Conducting periodic risk assessments and access reviews.

Ensuring compliance with industry regulations and internal security standards.

Automating policy enforcement to minimize human errors and security gaps.

Continuous improvement is essential in GRC for RBAC and ABAC. Organizations should regularly evaluate access policies, refine governance frameworks, and adopt emerging security best practices to ensure that access control mechanisms remain effective, scalable, and compliant. By aligning RBAC and ABAC with GRC objectives, businesses can enhance security, reduce operational risks, and ensure compliance with evolving regulatory landscapes.

Best Practices for Access Control Policy Management

Effective access control policy management is critical for securing sensitive systems, enforcing regulatory compliance, and ensuring that users have the appropriate level of access to perform their tasks. Poorly managed access control policies can lead to excessive permissions, unauthorized access, insider threats, and compliance violations. Organizations implementing Role-Based Access Control (RBAC) and Attribute-Based Access Control (ABAC) must follow best practices to ensure that access policies remain structured, scalable, and dynamically enforced across all IT environments, including on-premises, cloud, and hybrid infrastructures.

One of the foundational best practices in access control policy management is the principle of least privilege (PoLP). Users should be granted only the minimum access necessary to perform their job functions. Implementing least privilege reduces the attack surface by limiting the number of users with high-risk or sensitive permissions. Organizations should regularly review role assignments and access permissions to ensure that users are not accumulating unnecessary access rights over time.

Another critical best practice is role minimization and optimization in RBAC. Many organizations suffer from role explosion, where excessive numbers of roles make access control difficult to manage. To prevent this issue, organizations should:

Consolidate redundant roles by grouping users with similar job functions into broader categories.

Use hierarchical roles to avoid duplicating permissions for different levels within the same job function.

Implement role engineering to define standardized role templates that align with business processes.

ABAC introduces context-aware access control, allowing policies to adapt to real-time conditions. Organizations should ensure that ABAC policies are dynamically enforced based on user attributes, resource sensitivity, and environmental factors. Best practices for ABAC policy management include:

Defining clear attribute sources (e.g., HR systems, identity providers, and security monitoring tools) to maintain accurate and updated access control data.

Ensuring attribute consistency by synchronizing user, device, and environmental attributes across all access control systems.

Applying real-time policy evaluation to grant or deny access based on changing security conditions, such as location, network trust level, and device security posture.

Segregation of Duties (SoD) is a key access control best practice that prevents conflicts of interest and fraud by ensuring that no single user has excessive control over critical business processes. Organizations should:

Define SoD policies that separate high-risk tasks, such as ensuring that a user who can approve financial transactions cannot also initiate them.

Use automated SoD checks to detect policy violations in RBAC and ABAC configurations.

Conduct periodic SoD audits to verify that access policies remain aligned with organizational security requirements.

Access control policies must be consistently enforced across all IT environments. Organizations should implement centralized policy management to maintain uniform access rules across on-premises applications, cloud services, and third-party integrations. A unified access control framework ensures that security teams can:

Define and enforce policies centrally while applying them across multiple platforms.

Reduce policy fragmentation, which can lead to inconsistent access decisions and security gaps.

Improve compliance reporting by ensuring that all access control actions are logged and monitored in a centralized system.

Automating access control policy management enhances efficiency, scalability, and security enforcement. Organizations should leverage Identity Governance and Administration (IGA) tools, Privileged Access Management (PAM) solutions, and cloud identity providers to automate:

User role provisioning and deprovisioning to ensure that access permissions adjust dynamically when employees join, change roles, or leave the organization.

Access certification workflows that allow managers to periodically review and approve access rights.

Policy enforcement actions, such as revoking access when security conditions change or when users no longer require certain permissions.

Continuous monitoring and auditing of access control policies help detect misconfigurations, excessive permissions, and unauthorized access attempts. Best practices include:

Integrating access control logs with Security Information and Event Management (SIEM) solutions to monitor access anomalies.

Using machine learning-driven User Behavior Analytics (UBA) to detect deviations from normal access patterns.

Conducting access control penetration tests to identify vulnerabilities in RBAC and ABAC implementations.

Organizations should implement risk-based access control policies that dynamically adjust access permissions based on real-time risk assessments. Risk-based policies consider user behavior, device trust level, geolocation, and login anomalies to enforce adaptive security controls. For example:

If an employee logs in from an untrusted country, the system can enforce step-up authentication or deny access entirely.

If a user attempts to access high-risk financial data outside normal working hours, additional approval may be required.

Managing third-party and privileged access is another critical best practice in access control policy management. External vendors, contractors, and partners often require temporary access to corporate resources, but improper access control management can expose organizations to supply chain attacks and insider threats. Organizations should:

Use Just-In-Time (JIT) access control to grant temporary, time-limited access instead of long-term privileges.

Apply strict role-based access policies for third parties, ensuring they only access necessary systems.

Require multi-factor authentication (MFA) and session monitoring for privileged users accessing sensitive resources.

To maintain compliance with security regulations, organizations must align access control policies with industry standards such as GDPR, HIPAA, SOX, PCI DSS, and ISO 27001. Compliance best practices include:

Documenting access control policies and role assignments for auditability.

Ensuring that all access control decisions are logged and retained according to regulatory requirements.

Regularly updating policies to align with evolving security standards and legal requirements.

Training and awareness programs help employees understand the importance of access control policies and how they impact security. Organizations should:

Educate users on least privilege access and role-based security best practices.

Train security teams on policy enforcement, risk assessments, and compliance obligations.

Ensure that developers and DevOps teams follow secure access management guidelines when integrating applications and CI/CD pipelines.

By following these best practices, organizations can create a scalable, secure, and adaptive access control policy framework that minimizes security risks, ensures compliance, and provides effective governance over RBAC and ABAC implementations.

Building an Access Control Roadmap for Enterprises

Developing a comprehensive access control roadmap is essential for enterprises to ensure data security, regulatory compliance, and operational efficiency. Without a clear plan, organizations risk privilege mismanagement, security gaps, and excessive access rights that could lead to data breaches, insider threats, and compliance failures. A well-structured access control roadmap provides a strategic approach to managing identities, enforcing least privilege access, and integrating modern access control models such as Role-Based Access Control (RBAC), Attribute-Based Access Control (ABAC), and risk-based access policies.

The first step in building an access control roadmap is conducting a comprehensive access control assessment. Organizations must identify existing access control mechanisms, audit current permissions, and evaluate security gaps. Key assessment areas include:

User role evaluation: Reviewing existing RBAC implementations to identify excessive permissions, role conflicts, and potential privilege creep.

Access policy analysis: Assessing current access policies to ensure they align with business needs and regulatory requirements.

Third-party access review: Identifying external vendors, contractors, and partners with access to enterprise resources and assessing security controls.

Privilege escalation risks: Evaluating whether administrative access and privileged accounts are properly restricted and monitored.

Once the assessment phase is complete, enterprises must define their access control objectives and strategic priorities. These objectives should align with business goals, security policies, and regulatory frameworks. Common strategic priorities include:

Implementing least privilege access to reduce unnecessary permissions and minimize security risks.

Enhancing role management and automation by refining RBAC structures and integrating ABAC for dynamic access control.

Ensuring compliance with industry regulations such as GDPR, HIPAA, SOX, and PCI DSS through access governance and auditability.

Securing cloud and hybrid environments by implementing multi-cloud access policies, identity federation, and risk-based authentication.

To build an effective access control roadmap, enterprises must adopt a phased implementation strategy that enables gradual improvements while minimizing operational disruptions. The roadmap should be structured into the following phases:

Phase 1: Foundation and Governance

In this phase, enterprises establish the governance framework for access control. This includes:

Defining access control policies and role structures based on business needs and regulatory compliance requirements.

Establishing an Identity and Access Management (IAM) governance committee responsible for overseeing access control decisions.

Implementing access control automation tools to streamline role assignment, user provisioning, and policy enforcement.

Developing training programs to educate employees on secure access practices, least privilege access, and multi-factor authentication (MFA) enforcement.

Phase 2: Role Optimization and Attribute-Based Access Control (ABAC) Integration

Enterprises should optimize RBAC policies by reducing role redundancy, eliminating inactive roles, and consolidating permissions into well-defined access groups. Organizations should:

Conduct role mining and cleanup to remove unnecessary roles and simplify RBAC structures.

Introduce ABAC for dynamic access control that adjusts permissions based on real-time security conditions, user behavior, and risk levels.

Ensure attribute synchronization between HR systems, identity providers, and access control platforms to maintain policy accuracy.

Phase 3: Risk-Based Access Control and Adaptive Security

Organizations should move towards risk-aware access control models by integrating real-time security intelligence and behavioral analytics into their access policies. This includes:

Implementing continuous authentication to monitor user behavior and adjust permissions dynamically.

Enforcing conditional access policies, such as restricting access from high-risk locations or enforcing additional authentication for sensitive actions.

Integrating Security Information and Event Management (SIEM) tools to detect anomalies and automate responses to suspicious access attempts.

Phase 4: Just-In-Time (JIT) and Zero Trust Access

To further enhance security, enterprises should implement JIT access control, ensuring that elevated privileges are granted only when needed and automatically revoked after a set duration. Additionally, adopting a Zero Trust security model ensures that all access requests are continuously verified and evaluated based on context and risk.

Key actions include:

Deploying JIT access for privileged users to minimize the attack surface of administrator accounts.

Applying Zero Standing Privileges (ZSP) principles, ensuring no user retains excessive long-term permissions.

Implementing micro-segmentation to limit access to only required network resources.

Phase 5: Continuous Access Governance and Compliance

Access control policies must evolve continuously to meet changing business requirements, security threats, and compliance mandates. Organizations should:

Automate periodic access reviews to ensure that permissions remain aligned with job functions.

Conduct security audits and compliance assessments to validate that access control policies meet regulatory standards.

Implement user behavior analytics (UBA) to detect and respond to suspicious access patterns and privilege misuse.

Refine access policies using AI-driven identity governance tools to optimize permissions and reduce excessive access.

A successful access control roadmap requires cross-functional collaboration between IT, security, HR, compliance teams, and business leadership. Organizations should establish KPIs and metrics to measure the effectiveness of their access control strategy, including:

Reduction in excessive permissions over time.

Number of successful and unsuccessful access attempts to sensitive systems.

Time to approve and revoke access requests using automated workflows.

Audit readiness scores based on compliance with security frameworks.

As enterprises scale their access control strategies, they should continuously adapt to emerging threats, technological advancements, and regulatory changes. By following a structured access control roadmap, organizations can achieve a secure, compliant, and efficient access management framework that protects critical assets, data, and users.

Final Thoughts: The Future of RBAC/ABAC in Cybersecurity

As cybersecurity continues to evolve in response to increasingly sophisticated threats, the future of Role-Based Access Control (RBAC) and Attribute-Based Access Control (ABAC) in safeguarding enterprise systems and sensitive data is becoming more crucial than ever. While both RBAC and ABAC have long been foundational models for managing user access and ensuring least privilege, they must now adapt to the dynamic, complex, and highly interconnected nature of modern IT environments. The integration of RBAC and ABAC with emerging technologies, such as artificial intelligence (AI), machine learning (ML), and zero-trust security models, will significantly shape the next generation of access control systems.

RBAC has been the backbone of access control for decades due to its simplicity and ease of implementation. By assigning users to specific roles that are linked to certain permissions, organizations can streamline access management. However, traditional RBAC can be limiting when it comes to addressing the needs of a modern enterprise that requires dynamic, context-based access. While RBAC is still relevant, the future will require it to be more flexible and adaptive. Role explosion, a problem often associated with RBAC, will need to be addressed through role optimization and integration with ABAC to create more refined, context-aware policies that align access permissions with specific circumstances. The growing demand for cloud adoption, remote work solutions, and mobile access means that access control systems will need to handle more complex use cases that RBAC alone cannot address.

This is where ABAC comes into play. By using attributes (e.g., location, time of access, device health) as the basis for access decisions, ABAC provides a level of granularity and flexibility that RBAC cannot achieve. In the future, ABAC is expected to take on a more prominent role in addressing the challenges of multi-cloud environments, dynamic workflows, and regulatory compliance. By considering the full context surrounding an access request, ABAC allows organizations to make real-time, risk-based decisions that go beyond simple role assignments. For example, an employee working remotely may need additional authentication or be denied access if they are trying to access sensitive data from an untrusted device or network. As the enterprise landscape becomes increasingly hybrid and the need for contextual, adaptive security measures rises, ABAC will be essential in ensuring secure, dynamic access control.

The future of access control will increasingly focus on risk-based and adaptive models, where access decisions are made based on real-time risk assessments. With the rise of Zero Trust architectures, where implicit trust is eliminated and access must be continuously verified, RBAC and ABAC will need to be integrated into a continuous verification system. Zero Trust principles, including least privilege access, micro-segmentation, and behavioral analytics, will complement RBAC and ABAC policies to ensure that access is dynamically adjusted according to changing security conditions. A user may be granted access under typical conditions, but if unusual behavior is detected—such as accessing a system at an odd hour or from an unfamiliar location—their access may be restricted or subjected to additional authentication requirements. This integration will allow organizations to respond quickly to threats and prevent unauthorized access in real-time.

Another key development in the future of RBAC and ABAC is their integration with Artificial Intelligence (AI) and Machine Learning (ML). AI and ML have the potential to transform access control by enabling automated threat detection, real-time access decisions, and continuous learning. With AI-driven user behavior analytics, systems will be able to continuously monitor user actions and learn patterns of normal behavior. This learning can help identify deviations and anomalous behaviors that may indicate a compromised account or unauthorized activity. AI-powered systems will adjust RBAC and ABAC policies dynamically, automatically refining access control decisions based on changing user behaviors, device health, and risk factors. Over time, AI will help fine-tune access decisions, ensuring that policies evolve with the threat landscape without manual intervention.

As enterprises become more global, identity federation and cross-platform integration will also shape the future of RBAC and ABAC. The need for seamless access across multiple platforms, clouds, and third-party services means that federated identity management (FIM) will be essential. RBAC and ABAC policies must be enforced not only within an organization but also across external partners, contractors, and vendors who access company resources. The integration of third-party identity providers and the use of Single Sign-On (SSO) technologies will allow users to access a variety of systems without needing multiple logins, while RBAC and ABAC rules will ensure consistent enforcement of access control policies across all systems.

The regulatory landscape will continue to evolve, and access control models must adapt to new compliance requirements. The future will demand more advanced compliance auditing and reporting capabilities from RBAC and ABAC systems. These systems will need to generate detailed audit logs that provide granular insights into who accessed what data, when, and why. With the increasing complexity of regulatory frameworks like GDPR, HIPAA, and CCPA, organizations will rely on automated access control systems that track and report on compliance without manual intervention. RBAC and ABAC will become increasingly automated, with real-time reporting tools ensuring that organizations remain compliant even as regulations evolve.

The growth of the Internet of Things (IoT) and edge computing will also present new challenges and opportunities for RBAC and ABAC. With an increasing number of connected devices, access control will need to extend beyond traditional user devices and cover IoT endpoints such as smart sensors, cameras, and medical devices. ABAC's ability to use device attributes will be particularly valuable in this context, ensuring that only trusted and authorized devices are allowed to interact with enterprise systems and sensitive data. Similarly, edge computing environments will require access control systems to enforce policies based on local processing and data access while maintaining a centralized governance model.

The future of RBAC and ABAC is shaped by the need for more adaptive, scalable, and intelligent access control mechanisms. As enterprises increasingly rely on hybrid cloud environments, AI-driven analytics, and regulatory compliance, access control systems will have to evolve to support real-time, risk-aware, and context-sensitive policies. The integration of RBAC, ABAC, and Zero Trust principles will enable organizations to respond to emerging threats, enforce least privilege access, and comply with an ever-expanding regulatory landscape. As cybersecurity challenges continue to grow in complexity, RBAC and ABAC will be at the forefront of securing critical enterprise resources in an increasingly dynamic and interconnected world.

www.ingramcontent.com/pod-product-compliance
Lightning Source LLC
La Vergne TN
LVHW051234050326
832903LV00028B/2396